ULTIMATE

POCKET
BIBLE
TRIVIA

ULTIMATE POCKET BIBLE TRIVIA

QUESTIONS, PUZZLES & QUIZZES

TIMOTHY E. PARKER

© 2016 by Timothy E. Parker

Published by Revell
a division of Baker Publishing Group
PO Box 6287, Grand Rapids, MI 49516-6287
www.revellbooks.com

Spire edition published 2022
ISBN 978-0-8007-4203-4 (paperback)
ISBN 978-1-4934-3758-0 (ebook)

All material in this edition was published in 2016 by Revell in *The Official Bible Brilliant Trivia Book*.

Printed in the United States of America

Scripture quotations are from the King James Version of the Bible.

Baker Publishing Group publications use paper produced from sustainable forestry practices and post-consumer waste whenever possible.

22   23   24   25   26   27   28   7   6   5   4   3   2   1

Contents

Section 3: The Bible Brilliant Section   161

Section 4: The Bonus Section   197

Before You Begin

It is time to become brilliant in the knowledge of God's Word, the richness of the biblical past and the prophetic future. To get the true benefits of this book, you may have to go through it more than once. The goal is to challenge you in multiple ways, using multiple strategies and a wide array of exercises, puzzles, and quizzes, to get you to the highest level of Bible knowledge, a level I call Bible brilliant.

Joshua 1:8 states, "This book of the law shall not depart out of thy mouth; but thou shalt meditate therein day and night, that thou mayest observe to do according to all that is written therein: for then thou shalt make thy way prosperous, and then thou shalt have good success." Although this book uses clever games, word play, and trivia to increase your overall Bible knowledge, its goal is no trivial matter. It behooves every believer to know as much about the Lord and his Word as humanly possible. This book will be overwhelmingly helpful in that endeavor.

It is far more important for you to learn and know the information in the exercises than to complete the exercises quickly. In fact, I strongly recommend that you never time yourself in any challenge presented but take your time and focus on retaining correct answers.

This is an open-book book. That means you may use your own Bible to find answers. It is always a good thing to have the Good Book open, and you are never penalized in any way for referencing your own Bible as you seek answers to the hundreds of questions presented.

Some of the exercises are easy, and some are maddeningly difficult. However, they all have one purpose, and that is to teach the Word of God and bring you to the highest levels of Bible understanding and true knowledge.

SECTION 1

THE MUST-KNOW SECTION

This section deals with Bible information, facts, and questions and answers that you absolutely must know to become Bible brilliant. (Answers begin on page 224.)

All human discoveries seem to be made only for the purpose of confirming more and more strongly the truths contained in the sacred Scriptures.

Sir William Herschel

Do Not Be Fooled

This is a simple true or false test to get things started. Award yourself 10 points on the score card in the back of this book for each correct true or false answer. Complete the entire test before checking your answers.

1. _____ The phrase "This too shall pass" is in the Bible.

2. _____ Eve bit into the forbidden apple in the Garden of Eden.

3. _____ "Spare the rod, spoil the child" is a biblical teaching on child raising.

4. _____ "God works in mysterious ways" is from the book of Proverbs.

5. _____ One of the most-quoted Bible verses is "Cleanliness is next to godliness."

6. _____ Three wise men visited Jesus on the day of his birth.

7. _____ "The Little Drummer Boy" Christmas song is based on the boy drummer in Micah.

8. _____ According to the book that bears his name, Jonah was in the belly of a whale for three days and three nights.

9. _____ Satan took the form of a serpent when he tempted Eve in the Garden of Eden.

10. _____ "God helps those who help themselves" is in the book of Psalms.

11. _____ "Money is the root of all evil" is a classic Bible verse concerning placing money above God.

12. _____ Jesus Christ himself said, "To thine own self be true."

13. _____ The apostle Paul said, "Love the sinner, hate the sin."

14. _____ The wise men visited the baby Jesus in the manger.

15. _____ There was one set of the Ten Commandments given to Moses.

The Essentials

To be truly Bible brilliant, you must have a strong, fundamental knowledge of the basics of the Bible. You may retake the following quiz as often as necessary and record only your highest score on the score card. You earn 2 points per correct answer.

1. What is the Bible's very first verse?
2. Who was the mother of Jesus?
3. What garden was the home of Adam and Eve?
4. What type of creature tricked Eve into eating forbidden fruit?
5. What was the method of execution the Romans used to kill Jesus?
6. What are the wages of sin, according to the Bible?
7. What was the name of Moses's brother?
8. What crime did Cain commit?
9. Who was thrown into a den of lions?
10. Man was made in whose image?
11. How does the Lord's Prayer start?
12. What did Jesus use to feed five thousand people?
13. What part of Adam's body did God use to create Eve?
14. What is the only sin that cannot be forgiven?
15. From what substance did God create man?
16. The ark was built to save humankind from what disaster?

17. When accused of knowing Jesus, who denied him three times?

18. What was placed on the head of Jesus Christ before his crucifixion?

19. Who lied to God when questioned about the whereabouts of his brother?

20. The Ten Commandments were written on what material?

21. How many apostles followed Jesus?

22. Who was directed by an angel to go see the baby Jesus?

23. What is the second book of the Bible?

24. Before David became king, what was his occupation?

25. What is the first book of the Bible?

26. What is the first book of the New Testament?

27. How did David kill Goliath?

28. Where was the "wilderness" in which John the Baptist preached?

29. What was written at the top of Jesus's cross?

30. In what did Jesus sleep after his birth?

31. Who was willing to offer his son as a sacrifice to the Lord?

32. What was miraculous about Jesus's mother?

33. After Noah built the ark, for how many days and nights did it rain?

34. Who was placed in an ark of bulrushes and placed in a river by his mother?

35. What curious thing happened to Jonah?

36. How was Ruth related to Naomi?

37. To whom was Mary engaged when she became pregnant with Jesus?

38. What book of the Bible contains hymns written by David?

39. What animals drowned themselves in the sea when demons cast out by Jesus entered them?

40. What psalm begins, "The LORD is my shepherd"?

41. Who wrote the majority of the letters that form a large part of the New Testament?

42. What wicked things did Joseph's brothers do to him and to get rid of him?

43. Who was the father of King David?

44. Who was the father of Solomon?

45. What is the final book of the Bible?

46. What is the last word of the Bible?

47. How many individual books are in the Bible?

48. What humble act did Jesus do for his disciples at the Last Supper?

49. What was the name of Adam and Eve's first son?

50. How long did it take the Lord to make the heaven and the earth?

Books of the Bible

The following exercise will help you learn the precise order of all sixty-six books of the Holy Scriptures without fail. For each question, simply fill in the name of the Bible book in its proper place in the list.

After mastering this exercise, which may take several attempts, you will know not only the precise order of the books as they appear in the Bible but also such facts as the twentieth book is Proverbs and the forty-fifth book is Romans.

You will be filling in 186 various blanks for the sixty-six Bible books during this exercise. Award yourself 1 point per blank. You may do this exercise as many times as necessary and record only your best score.

1.

1. Genesis
2.
3. Leviticus
4.
5. Deuteronomy

2.

1.
2. Exodus
3. Leviticus
4. Numbers
5.

3.
1. Genesis
2. Exodus
3.
4. Numbers
5.

4.
1. Genesis
2.
3.
4. Numbers
5. Deuteronomy

5.
3. Leviticus
4.
5. Deuteronomy
6.
7. Judges
8. Ruth

6.
4. Numbers
5.
6. Joshua
7.
8.
9. 1 Samuel
10. 2 Samuel

7.
4. Numbers
5. Deuteronomy
6. Joshua
7.
8. Ruth
9.
10. 2 Samuel

8.
4. Numbers
5.
6. Joshua
7. Judges
8.
9. 1 Samuel
10.

9.
4. Numbers
5. Deuteronomy
6.
7. Judges
8.
9. 1 Samuel
10. 2 Samuel

10.

7. Judges
8.
9. 1 Samuel
10.
11. 1 Kings
12.
13. 1 Chronicles

11.

7. Judges
8. Ruth
9.
10. 2 Samuel
11.
12. 2 Kings
13.

12.

7. Judges
8. Ruth
9. 1 Samuel
10.
11. 1 Kings
12.
13. 1 Chronicles

13.

7. Judges
8.
9. 1 Samuel
10. 2 Samuel
11.
12. 2 Kings
13.

14.

11. 1 Kings
12.
13. 1 Chronicles
14. 2 Chronicles
15.
16. Nehemiah
17. Esther
18.
19. Psalms
20. Proverbs

15.

11. 1 Kings
12. 2 Kings
13. 1 Chronicles
14. 2 Chronicles
15.
16. Nehemiah
17.
18. Job
19.
20. Proverbs

16.

11. 1 Kings
12. 2 Kings
13. 1 Chronicles
14. 2 Chronicles
15. Ezra
16.
17. Esther
18. Job
19. Psalms
20.

17.

11. 1 Kings
12. 2 Kings
13. 1 Chronicles
14. 2 Chronicles
15.
16. Nehemiah
17. Esther
18.
19. Psalms
20.

18.

11. 1 Kings
12.
13. 1 Chronicles
14. 2 Chronicles
15.
16. Nehemiah
17.
18. Job
19. Psalms
20.

19.

11.
12. 2 Kings
13. 1 Chronicles
14. 2 Chronicles
15. Ezra
16.
17. Esther
18. Job
19.
20. Proverbs

20.

17.
18. Job
19. Psalms
20.
21. Ecclesiastes
22.
23. Isaiah
24. Jeremiah
25. Lamentations

21.

17. Esther
18. Job
19.
20. Proverbs
21.
22. Song of Solomon
23.
24. Jeremiah
25. Lamentations

22.

17.
18. Job
19. Psalms
20. Proverbs
21.
22. Song of Solomon
23. Isaiah
24.
25. Lamentations

23.

17. Esther
18.
19. Psalms
20. Proverbs
21. Ecclesiastes
22.
23. Isaiah
24. Jeremiah
25.

24.

20.
21. Ecclesiastes
22.
23. Isaiah
24. Jeremiah
25. Lamentations
26.
27. Daniel
28. Hosea
29.
30. Amos

25.

20. Proverbs
21. Ecclesiastes
22.
23. Isaiah
24. Jeremiah
25.
26. Ezekiel
27. Daniel
28. Hosea

29. Joel
30.

26.

20. Proverbs
21. Ecclesiastes
22. Song of Solomon
23.
24. Jeremiah
25. Lamentations
26.
27. Daniel
28.
29. Joel
30. Amos

27.

20.
21. Ecclesiastes
22. Song of Solomon
23. Isaiah
24.
25. Lamentations
26. Ezekiel
27.
28. Hosea
29. Joel
30.

28.

20. Proverbs
21. Ecclesiastes
22.
23. Isaiah

24. Jeremiah
25.
26. Ezekiel
27. Daniel
28. Hosea
29.
30. Amos

29.

20. Proverbs
21. Ecclesiastes
22. Song of Solomon
23.
24. Jeremiah
25. Lamentations
26.
27.
28. Hosea
29.
30. Amos

30.

20.
21. Ecclesiastes
22. Song of Solomon
23. Isaiah
24.
25. Lamentations
26. Ezekiel
27.
28. Hosea
29. Joel
30.

31.

26.
27. Daniel
28. Hosea
29.
30. Amos
31. Obadiah
32.
33. Micah
34.
35. Habakkuk

32.

26. Ezekiel
27. Daniel
28.
29. Joel
30. Amos
31.
32. Jonah
33.
34. Nahum
35. Habakkuk

33.

26.
27. Daniel
28. Hosea
29. Joel
30. Amos
31.
32. Jonah
33. Micah
34.
35. Habakkuk

34.

26. Ezekiel
27.
28. Hosea
29. Joel
30. Amos
31. Obadiah
32.
33. Micah
34. Nahum
35.

35.

30. Amos
31. Obadiah
32.
33. Micah
34. Nahum
35.
36. Zephaniah
37.
38. Zechariah
39. Malachi

36.

30. Amos
31. Obadiah
32. Jonah
33.
34. Nahum
35. Habakkuk
36.
37. Haggai
38. Zechariah
39.

37.

30. Amos
31.
32. Jonah
33. Micah
34.
35. Habakkuk
36. Zephaniah
37.
38. Zechariah
39.

38.

30. Amos
31. Obadiah
32.
33. Micah
34. Nahum
35.
36. Zephaniah
37.
38. Zechariah
39. Malachi

39.

30.
31. Obadiah
32. Jonah
33.
34. Nahum
35. Habakkuk
36.
37. Haggai
38.
39. Malachi

Fill in each of the twenty-seven books of the New Testament as necessary to create a perfect order.

40.

40. Matthew
41. Mark
42.
43. John
44. Acts (of the Apostles)

41.

40.
41. Mark
42. Luke
43.
44. Acts

42.

40. Matthew
41.
42. Luke
43. John
44.

43.

40. Matthew
41.
42. Luke
43.
44. Acts
45.
46.

47.
48. Galatians
49.
50. Philippians
51. Colossians
52. 1 Thessalonians

44.

43. John
44.
45. Romans
46. 1 Corinthians
47.
48. Galatians
49. Ephesians
50.

45.

43.
44.
45. Romans
46.
47. 2 Corinthians
48.
49. Ephesians
50. Philippians

46.

43. John
44. Acts
45.
46. 1 Corinthians
47. 2 Corinthians
48.

49. Ephesians
50. Philippians
51.
52. 1 Thessalonians
53.

47.

47.
48. Galatians
49.
50. Philippians
51.
52. 1 Thessalonians
53. 2 Thessalonians
54. 1 Timothy
55.
56. Titus

48.

49. Ephesians
50.
51. Colossians
52.
53. 2 Thessalonians

49.

49.
50. Philippians
51.
52. 1 Thessalonians
53. 2 Thessalonians
54. 1 Timothy
55. 2 Timothy

56.
57. Philemon
58.
59. James

50.

49. Ephesians
50.
51. Colossians
52. 1 Thessalonians
53.
54. 1 Timothy
55. 2 Timothy
56. Titus
57.
58. Hebrews
59.

51.

49.
50. Philippians
51. Colossians
52. 1 Thessalonians
53. 2 Thessalonians
54.
55.
56. Titus
57.
58. Hebrews
59.

52.

50.
51.
52. 1 Thessalonians
53. 2 Thessalonians
54. 1 Timothy
55. 2 Timothy
56.
57. Philemon
58. Hebrews
59.
60. 1 Peter

53.

53.
54. 1 Timothy
55. 2 Timothy
56. Titus
57.
58. Hebrews
59. James
60.

54.

50. Philippians
51. Colossians
52. 1 Thessalonians
53.
54. 1 Timothy
55.
56. Titus
57. Philemon
58.
59. James

55.

57. Philemon
58. Hebrews
59.
60. 1 Peter
61. 2 Peter
62.

56.

54. 1 Timothy
55.
56.
57. Philemon
58. Hebrews
59. James
60.
61. 2 Peter
62.

57.

61.
62. 1 John
63. 2 John
64.

58.

58.
59. James
60.
61. 2 Peter
62.
63. 2 John
64.
65. Jude

59.

59.
60. 1 Peter
61. 2 Peter
62. 1 John
63. 2 John
64. 3 John
65.
66. Revelation

60.

56.
57. Philemon
58.
59. James
60. 1 Peter
61.
62. 1 John
63. 2 John
64.
65. Jude
66.

Did You Know?

(SET 1)

Here is our first set of astonishing facts found by close study of the Holy Scriptures.

- The book of Esther is the only book in the Bible that does not mention the word *God*.
- The Israelites crossed the Red Sea at night, not during the day. The Lord created a "pillar" of a cloud to provide light for the Israelites, while the Egyptians saw only darkness (Exodus 14:19–22).
- There will be no marriages in heaven (Matthew 22:30; Mark 12:25; Luke 20:34–35).
- Luke 19:23 speaks about putting money in the bank to allow it to earn interest.
- Hebrews 13:2 instructs us to always show hospitality to strangers because we may unknowingly be helping an angel.
- Although Joshua wrote the book of Joshua, he could not have written Joshua 24:29–33, which describes his death and Israel after his death.

5

150 Key Verses

Knowing key Scripture passages is essential to becoming a Bible scholar. In this important exercise, you are given 150 verses with one key word missing. If you fill in the missing word correctly, you may reward yourself with 2 points.

1. John 3:16
   For God so loved the world that he gave his only begotten Son, that whosoever _____ in him should not perish, but have everlasting life.

2. John 1:1
   In the beginning was the _____, and the Word was with God, and the Word was God.

3. John 14:6
   Jesus saith unto him, I am the way, the truth, and the life: no man cometh unto the _____, but by me.

4. Matthew 28:19
   Go ye therefore, and teach all _____, baptizing them in the name of the Father, and of the Son, and of the Holy Ghost.

5. Romans 3:23
   For all have _____, and come short of the glory of God.

6. Ephesians 2:8

   For by _____ are ye saved through faith; and that not of yourselves: it is the gift of God.

7. Genesis 1:1

   In the _____ God created the heaven and the earth.

8. Acts 1:8

   But ye shall receive _____, after that the Holy Ghost is come upon you: and ye shall be witnesses unto me both in Jerusalem, and in all Judaea, and in Samaria, and unto the uttermost part of the earth.

9. 2 Timothy 3:16

   _____ scripture is given by inspiration of God, and is profitable for doctrine, for reproof, for correction, for instruction in righteousness.

10. Romans 10:9

    That if thou shalt confess with thy mouth the Lord _____, and shalt believe in thine heart that God hath raised him from the dead, thou shalt be saved.

11. Romans 6:23

    For the wages of sin is _____; but the gift of God is eternal life through Jesus Christ our Lord.

12. Acts 2:38

    Then Peter said unto them, _____, and be baptized every one of you in the name of Jesus Christ for the remission of sins, and ye shall receive the gift of the Holy Ghost.

13. John 1:12

    But as many as received him, to them gave he power to become the sons of God, even to them that _____ on his name.

14. Romans 8:28
    And we know that all things work together for _____ to them that love God, to them who are the called according to his purpose.

15. John 1:9
    That was the true _____, which lighteth every man that cometh into the world.

16. Genesis 1:26
    And God said, Let us make man in our _____, after our likeness: and let them have dominion over the fish of the sea, and over the fowl of the air, and over the cattle, and over all the earth, and over every creeping thing that creepeth upon the earth.

17. Romans 12:1
    I beseech you therefore, brethren, by the mercies of God, that ye present your _____ a living sacrifice, holy, acceptable unto God, which is your reasonable service.

18. Romans 5:8
    But God commendeth his love toward us, in that, while we were yet _____, Christ died for us.

19. Matthew 28:18
    And Jesus came and spake unto them, saying, All _____ is given unto me in heaven and in earth.

20. John 3:3
    Jesus answered and said unto him, Verily, verily, I say unto thee, Except a man be _____ again, he cannot see the kingdom of God.

21. Mark 16:15

    And he said unto them, Go ye into all the world, and preach the _____ to every creature.

22. John 10:10

    The _____ cometh not, but for to steal, and to kill, and to destroy: I am come that they might have life, and that they might have it more abundantly.

23. John 1:14

    And the _____ was made flesh, and dwelt among us, (and we beheld his glory, the glory as of the only begotten of the Father,) full of grace and truth.

24. Acts 4:12

    Neither is there _____ in any other: for there is none other name under heaven given among men, whereby we must be saved.

25. Acts 2:42

    And they continued stedfastly in the apostles' doctrine and fellowship, and in breaking of bread, and in _____.

26. Galatians 5:22

    But the fruit of the _____ is love, joy, peace, longsuffering, gentleness, goodness, faith.

27. Proverbs 3:5

    _____ in the LORD with all thine heart; and lean not unto thine own understanding.

28. Jeremiah 29:11

    For I know the thoughts that I think toward you, saith the LORD, thoughts of peace, and not of _____, to give you an expected end.

29. Titus 3:5

    Not by works of righteousness which we have done, but
    according to his mercy he _____ us, by the washing
    of regeneration, and renewing of the Holy Ghost.

30. Romans 12:2

    And be not conformed to this _____: but be ye
    transformed by the renewing of your mind, that ye may
    prove what is that good, and acceptable, and perfect, will
    of God.

31. John 14:1

    Let not your heart be _____: ye believe in God,
    believe also in me.

32. John 4:1

    When therefore the Lord knew how the Pharisees had
    heard that Jesus made and _____ more disciples than
    John.

33. Ephesians 4:11

    And he gave some, apostles; and some, prophets; and
    some, _____; and some, pastors and teachers.

34. Romans 5:12

    Wherefore, as by one man _____ entered into the
    world, and death by sin; and so death passed upon all
    men, for that all have sinned.

35. Matthew 11:28

    Come unto me, all ye that labour and are heavy laden, and
    I will give you _____.

36. Romans 5:1

    Therefore being justified by _____, we have peace
    with God through our Lord Jesus Christ.

37. Genesis 1:27

    So God _____ man in his own image, in the image of
    God created he him; male and female created he them.

38. Romans 1:16

    For I am not ashamed of the _____ of Christ: for
    it is the power of God unto salvation to every one that
    believeth; to the Jew first, and also to the Greek.

39. 1 John 1:9

    If we confess our sins, he is faithful and just to forgive us
    our sins, and to _____ us from all unrighteousness.

40. Acts 2:1

    And when the day of _____ was fully come, they
    were all with one accord in one place.

41. 2 Corinthians 5:17

    Therefore if any man be in _____, he is a new
    creature: old things are passed away; behold, all things are
    become new.

42. Hebrews 11:1

    Now _____ is the substance of things hoped for, the
    evidence of things not seen.

43. 2 Timothy 2:15

    Study to shew thyself _____ unto God, a workman
    that needeth not to be ashamed, rightly dividing the word
    of truth.

44. Romans 8:1

    There is therefore now no _____ to them which are
    in Christ Jesus, who walk not after the flesh, but after the
    Spirit.

45. Romans 10:13
   For whosoever shall call upon the name of the Lord shall
   be _____.

46. John 8:32
   And ye shall know the truth, and the truth shall make you
   _____.

47. Isaiah 9:6
   For unto us a child is born, unto us a son is given: and the
   _____ shall be upon his shoulder: and his name shall
   be called Wonderful, Counsellor, The mighty God, The
   everlasting Father, The Prince of Peace.

48. John 14:15
   If ye _____ me, keep my commandments.

49. Deuteronomy 6:4
   Hear, O Israel: The LORD our God is _____ LORD.

50. John 13:34
   A new _____ I give unto you, That ye love one
   another; as I have loved you, that ye also love one another.

51. John 4:24
   God is a Spirit: and they that worship him must worship
   him in spirit and in _____.

52. Philippians 4:13
   I can do all things through _____ which
   strengtheneth me.

53. Ephesians 2:1
   And you hath he quickened, who were dead in trespasses
   and _____.

54. John 14:16

And I will pray the _____, and he shall give you another Comforter, that he may abide with you for ever.

55. Genesis 1:2

And the earth was without form, and void; and _____ was upon the face of the deep. And the Spirit of God moved upon the face of the waters.

56. Hebrews 4:12

For the word of God is quick, and powerful, and sharper than any twoedged sword, piercing even to the dividing asunder of soul and _____, and of the joints and marrow, and is a discerner of the thoughts and intents of the heart.

57. James 5:16

_____ your faults one to another, and pray one for another, that ye may be healed. The effectual fervent prayer of a righteous man availeth much.

58. Isaiah 7:14

Therefore the Lord himself shall give you a sign; Behold, a _____ shall conceive, and bear a son, and shall call his name Immanuel.

59. John 1:7

The same came for a witness, to bear witness of the Light, that all men through him might _____.

60. John 3:5

Jesus answered, Verily, verily, I say unto thee, Except a man be born of _____ and of the Spirit, he cannot enter into the kingdom of God.

61. Philippians 2:5

    Let this _____ be in you, which was also in Christ Jesus.

62. John 1:29

    The next day John seeth Jesus coming unto him, and saith, Behold the Lamb of God, which taketh away the _____ of the world.

63. Romans 1:18

    For the _____ of God is revealed from heaven against all ungodliness and unrighteousness of men, who hold the truth in unrighteousness.

64. Philippians 4:6

    Be careful for _____; but in every thing by prayer and supplication with thanksgiving let your requests be made known unto God.

65. Hebrews 12:1

    Wherefore seeing we also are compassed about with so great a cloud of _____, let us lay aside every weight, and the sin which doth so easily beset us, and let us run with patience the race that is set before us.

66. John 1:3

    All things were _____ by him; and without him was not any thing made that was made.

67. Matthew 16:18

    And I say also unto thee, That thou art Peter, and upon this _____ I will build my church; and the gates of hell shall not prevail against it.

68. Galatians 2:20

    I am _____ with Christ: nevertheless I live; yet not I, but Christ liveth in me: and the life which I now live in the flesh I live by the faith of the Son of God, who loved me, and gave himself for me.

69. Matthew 25:31

    When the Son of man shall come in his glory, and all the holy angels with him, then shall he sit upon the _____ of his glory.

70. Matthew 5:17

    Think not that I am come to destroy the law, or the prophets: I am not come to destroy, but to _____.

71. Romans 10:17

    So then _____ cometh by hearing, and hearing by the word of God.

72. Matthew 6:33

    But seek ye first the kingdom of God, and his _____; and all these things shall be added unto you.

73. Luke 4:18

    The _____ of the Lord is upon me, because he hath anointed me to preach the gospel to the poor; he hath sent me to heal the brokenhearted, to preach deliverance to the captives, and recovering of sight to the blind, to set at liberty them that are bruised.

74. John 16:13

    Howbeit when he, the Spirit of _____, is come, he will guide you into all truth: for he shall not speak of himself; but whatsoever he shall hear, that shall he speak: and he will shew you things to come.

75. Acts 20:28

    Take heed therefore unto yourselves, and to all the flock,
    over the which the Holy Ghost hath made you overseers,
    to feed the church of God, which he hath purchased with
    his own _____.

76. Titus 2:11

    For the grace of God that bringeth _____ hath
    appeared to all men.

77. John 8:44

    Ye are of your father the devil, and the lusts of your father
    ye will do. He was a murderer from the beginning, and
    abode not in the _____, because there is no truth in
    him. When he speaketh a lie, he speaketh of his own: for
    he is a liar, and the father of it.

78. Ephesians 6:10

    Finally, my brethren, be strong in the Lord, and in the
    _____ of his might.

79. Romans 13:1

    Let every soul be subject unto the higher powers. For
    there is no power but of _____: the powers that be
    are ordained of God.

80. John 2:15

    And when he had made a scourge of small cords, he drove
    them all out of the temple, and the sheep, and the oxen;
    and poured out the changers' money, and overthrew the

    _____.

81. Mark 16:16

    He that believeth and is _____ shall be saved; but he
    that believeth not shall be damned.

82. Romans 3:10

    As it is written, There is none _____, no, not one.

83. Genesis 3:15

    And I will put enmity between thee and the _____, and between thy seed and her seed; it shall bruise thy head, and thou shalt bruise his heel.

84. Hebrews 11:6

    But without _____ it is impossible to please him: for he that cometh to God must believe that he is, and that he is a rewarder of them that diligently seek him.

85. John 14:26

    But the Comforter, which is the Holy Ghost, whom the _____ will send in my name, he shall teach you all things, and bring all things to your remembrance, whatsoever I have said unto you.

86. John 5:24

    Verily, verily, I say unto you, He that heareth my word, and believeth on him that sent me, hath everlasting life, and shall not come into condemnation; but is passed from _____ unto life.

87. Joel 2:28

    And it shall come to pass afterward, that I will pour out my _____ upon all flesh; and your sons and your daughters shall prophesy, your old men shall dream dreams, your young men shall see visions.

88. Genesis 1:11

    And God said, Let the earth bring forth grass, the herb yielding seed, and the fruit tree yielding fruit after his _____, whose seed is in itself, upon the earth: and it was so.

89. James 1:2
    My brethren, count it all _____ when ye fall into
    divers temptations.

90. Colossians 1:15
    Who is the image of the invisible God, the _____ of
    every creature.

91. Matthew 22:37
    Jesus said unto him, Thou shalt love the Lord thy God
    with all thy heart, and with all thy soul, and with all thy
    _____.

92. Titus 2:13
    Looking for that blessed _____, and the glorious
    appearing of the great God and our Saviour Jesus Christ.

93. Philippians 4:8
    Finally, brethren, whatsoever things are true, whatsoever
    things are honest, whatsoever things are just, what-
    soever things are pure, whatsoever things are lovely,
    whatsoever things are of good report; if there be any vir-
    tue, and if there be any _____, think on these things.

94. Acts 1:9
    And when he had spoken these things, while they beheld,
    he was taken up; and a _____ received him out of
    their sight.

95. John 4:7
    There cometh a woman of _____ to draw water: Jesus
    saith unto her, Give me to drink.

96. Micah 6:8
    He hath shewed thee, O man, what is good; and what
    doth the LORD require of thee, but to do justly, and to
    love mercy, and to walk _____ with thy God?

97. John 17:17

      _____ them through thy truth: thy word is truth.

98. Acts 20:7

    And upon the first day of the week, when the disciples
    came together to break bread, _____ preached unto
    them, ready to depart on the morrow; and continued his
    speech until midnight.

99. Acts 16:31

    And they said, Believe on the Lord Jesus Christ, and thou
    shalt be saved, and thy _____.

100. John 11:25

     Jesus said unto her, I am the _____, and the life: he
     that believeth in me, though he were dead, yet shall he
     live.

101. John 8:58

     Jesus said unto them, Verily, verily, I say unto you, Before
     _____ was, I am.

102. Acts 2:4

     And they were all filled with the Holy Ghost, and began
     to speak with other _____, as the Spirit gave them
     utterance.

103. John 15:5

     I am the vine, ye are the _____: He that abideth in
     me, and I in him, the same bringeth forth much fruit: for
     without me ye can do nothing.

104. Acts 2:41

     Then they that gladly received his word were _____:
     and the same day there were added unto them about three
     thousand souls.

105. Proverbs 22:6

Train up a _____ in the way he should go: and when he is old, he will not depart from it.

106. Genesis 3:1

Now the _____ was more subtil than any beast of the field which the Lord God had made. And he said unto the woman, Yea, hath God said, Ye shall not eat of every tree of the garden?

107. James 1:5

If any of you lacks _____, let him ask of God, that giveth to all men liberally, and upbraideth not; and it shall be given him.

108. Hebrews 1:1

God, who at sundry times and in divers manners spake in time past unto the fathers by the _____.

109. 2 John 1:2

For the _____ sake, which dwelleth in us, and shall be with us for ever.

110. John 17:3

And this is life _____, that they might know thee the only true God, and Jesus Christ, whom thou hast sent.

111. John 5:7

The impotent man answered him, Sir, I have no man, when the _____ is troubled, to put me into the pool: but while I am coming, another steppeth down before me.

112. John 8:31

Then said Jesus to those Jews which believed on him, If ye continue in my word, then are ye my _____ indeed.

113. Luke 1:4

That thou mightest know the certainty of those things, wherein thou hast been _____.

114. Revelation 3:20

Behold, I stand at the door, and knock: if any man hear my _____, and open the door, I will come in to him, and will sup with him, and he with me.

115. 1 Peter 2:3

If so be ye have _____ that the Lord is gracious.

116. John 10:30

I and my _____ are one.

117. 1 Peter 3:15

But sanctify the Lord God in your hearts: and be ready always to give an answer to every man that asketh you a reason of the _____ that is in you with meekness and fear.

118. Matthew 7:21

Not every one that saith unto me, Lord, Lord, shall enter into the kingdom of heaven; but he that doeth the _____ of my Father which is in heaven.

119. John 3:18

He that believeth on him is not condemned: but he that believeth not is condemned already, because he hath not believed in the name of the only _____ Son of God.

120. Genesis 12:1

Now the LORD had said unto _____, Get thee out of thy country, and from thy kindred, and from thy father's house, unto a land that I will shew thee.

121. John 3:8

    The wind bloweth where it listeth, and thou hearest the sound thereof, but canst not tell whence it cometh, and whither it goeth: so is every one that is born of the _____.

122. John 15:1

    I am the true _____, and my Father is the husbandman.

123. Genesis 2:7

    And the LORD God formed man of the dust of the ground, and breathed into his nostrils the breath of _____; and man became a living soul.

124. Genesis 1:3

    And God said, _____ there be light: and there was light.

125. John 8:12

    Then spake Jesus again unto them, saying, I am the _____ of the world: he that followeth me shall not walk in darkness, but shall have the light of life.

126. 1 Peter 2:9

    But ye are a _____ generation, a royal priesthood, an holy nation, a peculiar people; that ye should shew forth the praises of him who hath called you out of darkness into his marvellous light.

127. Luke 1:26

    And in the _____ month the angel Gabriel was sent from God unto a city of Galilee, named Nazareth.

128. Hebrews 9:27

    And as it is appointed unto men once to die, but after this the _____.

129. John 3:2

     The same came to Jesus by night, and said unto him,
     _____, we know that thou art a teacher come from
     God: for no man can do these miracles that thou doest,
     except God be with him.

130. Matthew 5:14

     Ye are the _____ of the world. A city that is set on an
     hill cannot be hid.

131. Exodus 3:14

     And God said unto _____, I Am That I Am: and he
     said, Thus shalt thou say unto the children of Israel, I Am
     hath sent me unto you.

132. 1 Corinthians 6:9

     Know ye not that the unrighteous shall not inherit the
     kingdom of God? Be not _____: neither fornicators,
     nor idolaters, nor adulterers, nor effeminate, nor abusers
     of themselves with mankind.

133. Luke 10:25

     And, behold, a certain lawyer stood up, and tempted
     him, saying, Master, what shall I do to inherit eternal
     _____?

134. Matthew 7:7

     _____, and it shall be given you; seek, and ye shall
     find; knock, and it shall be opened unto you.

135. Ephesians 1:3

     _____ be the God and Father of our Lord Jesus
     Christ, who hath blessed us with all spiritual blessings in
     heavenly places in Christ.

136. Matthew 1:18

     Now the _____ of Jesus Christ was on this wise:
     When as his mother Mary was espoused to Joseph, before
     they came together, she was found with child of the Holy
     Ghost.

137. Romans 1:20

     For the invisible things of him from the creation of the
     world are clearly seen, being understood by the things
     that are made, even his eternal power and Godhead; so
     that they are without _____.

138. John 8:9

     And they which heard it, being convicted by their own
     conscience, went out one by one, beginning at the eldest,
     even unto the last: and _____ was left alone, and the
     woman standing in the midst.

139. John 1:5

     And the _____ shineth in darkness; and the darkness
     comprehended it not.

140. 1 Thessalonians 4:13

     But I would not have you to be ignorant, brethren,
     concerning them which are asleep, that ye sorrow not,
     even as others which have no _____.

141. Hebrews 13:5

     Let your conversation be without covetousness; and be
     content with such things as ye have: for he hath said, I will
     never leave thee, nor _____ thee.

142. 1 John 4:1

     Beloved, believe not every _____, but try the spirits
     whether they are of God: because many false prophets are
     gone out into the world.

143. James 1:17

    Every good _____ and every perfect gift is from
    above, and cometh down from the Father of lights, with
    whom is no variableness, neither shadow of turning.

144. Matthew 6:19

    Lay not up for yourselves _____ upon earth, where
    moth and rust doth corrupt, and where thieves break
    through and steal.

145. Isaiah 61:1

    The Spirit of the Lord GOD is upon me; because the
    LORD hath anointed me to _____ good tidings unto
    the meek; he hath sent me to bind up the brokenhearted,
    to proclaim liberty to the captives, and the opening of the
    prison to them that are bound.

146. Galatians 3:28

    There is neither Jew nor Greek, there is neither bond
    nor free, there is neither male nor female: for ye are all
    _____ in Christ Jesus.

147. 2 Peter 3:9

    The Lord is not slack concerning his _____, as some
    men count slackness; but is longsuffering to us-ward, not
    willing that any should perish, but that all should come to
    repentance.

148. Acts 1:11

    Which also said, Ye men of Galilee, why stand ye gazing
    up into heaven? this same _____, which is taken up
    from you into heaven, shall so come in like manner as ye
    have seen him go into heaven.

149. James 5:14

  Is any _____ among you? let him call for the elders
  of the church; and let them pray over him, anointing him
  with oil in the name of the Lord.

150. John 3:36

  He that believeth on the _____ hath everlasting life:
  and he that believeth not the Son shall not see life; but the
  wrath of God abideth on him.

ALL ABOUT MONEY

In the following exercises that teach God's wisdom in money affairs, take the words under each Scripture passage and put them in the appropriate blanks. By studying which word goes into which blank, you will learn what God desires us to know about money. Give yourself 2 points for each passage you complete accurately.

Any repeats of passages throughout the various money topics are intentional.

Maintaining Budgets

1. Proverbs 6:6–8
   Go to the ant, thou _____; consider her ways, and be wise: Which having no _____, overseer, or ruler, Provideth her meat in the summer, and gathereth her food in the _____.

   guide   sluggard   harvest

2. Proverbs 21:5
   The _____ of the _____ tend only to plenteousness; but of every one that is _____ only to want.

   diligent   hasty   thoughts

3. Proverbs 22:3
   A prudent man _____ the evil, and _____ himself: but the _____ pass on, and are _____.

   punished   simple   foreseeth   hideth

4. Proverbs 24:3–4
   Through _____ is an house builded; and by understanding it is established: And by _____ shall the _____ be _____ with all precious and _____ riches.

   pleasant   wisdom   knowledge   chambers   filled

5. Proverbs 25:28

   He that hath no _____ over his own _____ is like
   a _____ that is broken down, and without _____.

   spirit   rule   walls   city

6. Proverbs 27:12 (This passage is nearly identical to the one
   in number 3, Proverbs 22:3. Their close proximity to each
   other in the Bible indicates that this is a vitally important
   idea.)

   A _____ man foreseeth the _____, and hideth
   _____; but the simple _____ on, and are
   punished.

   evil   prudent   pass   himself

7. Proverbs 27:23

   Be thou _____ to know the state of thy _____,
   and _____ well to thy _____.

   look   flocks   herds   diligent

8. Proverbs 27:26

   The _____ are for thy _____, and the goats are
   the _____ of the _____.

   price   field   clothing   lambs

9. Luke 14:28–30

   For which of you, intending to _____ a _____,
   sitteth not down first, and counteth the cost, whether
   he have sufficient to _____ it? Lest haply, after he
   hath laid the _____, and is not able to finish it, all
   that behold it begin to _____ him, Saying, This man
   began to build, and was not able to finish.

   finish   tower   build   foundation   mock

10. 1 Corinthians 16:2

Upon the first day of the _____ let every one of you _____ by him in store, as God hath _____ him, that there be no _____ when I come.

prospered   week   gatherings   lay

Debt

1. Exodus 22:14
   And if a man _____ ought of his neighbour, and it be
   _____, or _____, the owner thereof being not
   with it, he shall surely make it _____.

   hurt   die   good   borrow

2. Deuteronomy 15:6
   For the LORD thy God blesseth thee, as he _____
   thee: and thou shalt lend unto many _____, but thou
   shalt not _____; and thou shalt _____ over many
   nations, but they shall not reign over thee.

   reign   nations   promised   borrow

3. Deuteronomy 28:12
   The LORD shall open unto thee his good _____, the
   _____ to give the rain unto thy land in his _____,
   and to bless all the work of thine _____: and thou
   shalt lend unto many _____, and thou shalt not
   borrow.

   season   heaven   nations   hand   treasure

4. 2 Kings 4:7
   Then she came and told the man of _____. And he
   said, Go, sell the _____, and pay thy _____, and
   live thou and thy _____ of the rest.

   debt   children   oil   God

5. Psalm 37:21

The wicked borroweth, and _____ not again: but the
_____ sheweth _____, and giveth.

    payeth   righteous   mercy

6. Proverbs 22:7

The _____ ruleth over the _____, and the
_____ is servant to the _____.

    poor   lender   borrower   rich

7. Proverbs 22:26–27

Be not thou one of them that strike _____, or of them
that are _____ for _____. If thou hast _____
to pay, why should he take away thy _____ from
under thee?

    sureties   bed   nothing   hands   debts

8. Ecclesiastes 5:5

_____ is it that thou shouldest not _____, than
that thou shouldest vow and not _____.

    pay   vow   better

9. Romans 13:8

Owe no _____ any thing, but to love one _____:
for he that loveth another hath fulfilled the _____.

    law   another   man

Wealth

1. Exodus 23:12
   Six days thou shalt do thy work, and on the _____ day thou shalt rest: that thine _____ and thine ass may rest, and the son of thy _____, and the _____, may be _____.

   refreshed   handmaid   ox   stranger   seventh

2. Proverbs 12:11
   He that tilleth his _____ shall be satisfied with _____: but he that followeth _____ persons is _____ of understanding.

   vain   void   land   bread

3. Proverbs 13:11
   _____ gotten by _____ shall be _____: but he that gathereth by labour shall _____.

   increase   vanity   diminished   wealth

4. Proverbs 14:15
   The _____ believeth every _____: but the prudent _____ looketh _____ to his going.

   man   simple   word   well

5. Proverbs 19:2

Also, that the soul be without _____, it is not
_____; and he that hasteth with his _____
_____.

feet   sinneth   knowledge   good

6. Proverbs 21:5

The _____ of the _____ _____ only to
plenteousness; but of _____ one that is _____
only to want.

diligent   hasty   thoughts   tend   every

7. Proverbs 23:4

_____ not to be _____: cease from _____
own _____.

rich   wisdom   thine   labour

8. Proverbs 28:19–20

He that tilleth his land shall have plenty of _____:
but he that followeth after _____ persons shall have
_____ enough. A faithful man shall abound with
blessings: but he that maketh haste to be _____ shall
not be _____.

innocent   poverty   vain   bread   rich

Did You Know?

(SET 2)

Here are more interesting facts from the Holy Scriptures.

- A ball is mentioned only once in the Bible. It occurs in Isaiah 22:18.
- When the Israelites wandered in the desert for forty years, God supernaturally prevented their clothes and sandals from wearing out (Deuteronomy 29:5).
- God actually sings (Zephaniah 3:17).
- When the dove released by Noah returned to the ark, it did not return with an olive branch. It was an olive leaf (Genesis 8:11).
- According to Matthew 22:15–16, the Pharisees had their own disciples.
- Abraham not only had a son with his wife, Sarah, but also had several sons with his concubine (Genesis 25:6).

10

Being Happy with What You Have

1. Psalm 23:1
   The _____ is my _____; I shall not _____.

   shepherd   want   LORD

2. Ecclesiastes 5:10
   He that loveth _____ shall not be satisfied with silver;
   nor he that loveth _____ with _____: this is also
   _____.

   vanity   silver   increase   abundance

3. Matthew 6:31–33
   Therefore take no _____, saying, What shall we eat?
   or, What shall we _____? or, Wherewithal shall we be
   _____? (For after all these things do the _____
   seek:) for your heavenly Father knoweth that ye have
   need of all these things. But seek ye first the kingdom
   of God, and his _____; and all these things shall be
   added unto you.

   clothed   Gentiles   righteousness   drink   thought

4. Luke 3:14
   And the _____ likewise demanded of him, saying,
   And what shall we do? And he said unto them, Do
   _____ to no man, neither accuse any _____; and
   be content with your _____.

   wages   falsely   violence   soldiers

5. Philippians 4:11–13

   Not that I speak in respect of want: for I have learned, in whatsoever _____ I am, therewith to be _____. I know both how to be abased, and I know how to abound: every where and in all things I am _____ both to be full and to be _____, both to abound and to suffer need. I can do all things through _____ which strengtheneth me.

   content   hungry   state   instructed   Christ

6. 1 Thessalonians 4:11

   And that ye study to be _____, and to do your own _____, and to work with your own _____, as we _____ you.

   quiet   business   commanded   hands

7. 1 Timothy 6:6

   But _____ with _____ is great _____.

   gain   godliness   contentment

8. 1 Timothy 6:7–10

   For we brought nothing into this world, and it is certain we can carry nothing out. And having food and _____ let us be therewith content. But they that will be rich fall into temptation and a snare, and into many _____ and hurtful _____, which drown men in _____ and perdition. For the love of money is the root of all evil: which while some coveted after, they have erred from the _____, and pierced themselves through with many _____.

   faith   raiment   lusts   foolish   destruction   sorrows

9. Hebrews 13:5

Let your _____ be without covetousness; and be content with such things as ye have: for he hath said, I will _____ leave thee, nor _____ thee.

forsake   conversation   never

10. James 4:1–3

From whence come _____ and fightings among you? come they not hence, even of your lusts that _____ in your _____? Ye lust, and have not: ye kill, and desire to have, and cannot obtain: ye fight and war, yet ye have not, because ye ask not. Ye _____, and receive not, because ye ask amiss, that ye may _____ it upon your lusts.

consume   ask   members   wars   war

Giving and Being Generous

1. Deuteronomy 15:10
   Thou shalt surely give him, and thine _____ shall not
   be grieved when thou givest unto him: because that for
   this thing the _____ thy God shall _____ thee
   in all thy _____, and in all that thou puttest thine
   _____ unto.

   hand   bless   works   heart   LORD

2. Deuteronomy 16:17
   Every _____ shall give as he is able, according to the
   _____ of the LORD thy _____ which he hath
   given _____.

   thee   man   God   blessing

3. 1 Chronicles 29:9
   Then the _____ rejoiced, for that they offered
   willingly, because with perfect _____ they offered
   willingly to the _____: and _____ the _____
   also rejoiced with great joy.

   LORD   David   people   heart   king

4. Proverbs 3:9–10
   Honour the LORD with thy _____, and with the
   _____ of all thine increase: So shall thy _____ be
   filled with plenty, and thy _____ shall burst out with
   new _____.

   presses   firstfruits   wine   substance   barns

5. Proverbs 3:27

   Withhold not _____ from them to whom it
   is _____, when it is in the _____ of thine
   _____ to do it.

   > hand   power   good   due

6. Proverbs 11:24–25

   There is that _____, and yet _____; and there
   is that withholdeth more than is meet, but it tendeth to
   poverty. The liberal _____ shall be made _____:
   and he that watereth shall be _____ also himself.

   > increaseth   fat   scattereth   soul   watered

7. Proverbs 21:26

   He _____ _____ all the _____ long: but the
   righteous giveth and _____ not.

   > day   coveteth   spareth   greedily

8. Proverbs 22:9

   He that hath a bountiful _____ shall be _____;
   for he giveth of his _____ to the _____.

   > bread   poor   eye   blessed

9. Proverbs 28:27

   He that giveth unto the _____ shall not _____: but
   he that hideth his _____ shall have many a _____.

   > lack   eyes   curse   poor

10. Malachi 3:10

    Bring ye all the tithes into the _____, that there may
    be meat in mine house, and prove me now herewith, saith
    the _____ of _____, if I will not open you the
    windows of heaven, and pour you out a _____, that
    there shall not be _____ enough to receive it.

    > blessing   storehouse   hosts   room   LORD

11. Matthew 6:3–4

But when thou doest _____, let not thy left _____ know what thy right hand doeth: That thine alms may be in _____: and thy _____ which seeth in secret himself shall reward _____ openly.

secret   alms   Father   thee   hand

12. Mark 12:41–44

And Jesus sat over against the _____, and beheld how the people _____ money into the treasury: and many that were rich cast in much. And there came a certain poor widow, and she threw in two mites, which make a farthing. And he called unto him his disciples, and saith unto them, Verily I say unto you, That this poor widow hath cast more in, than all they which have cast into the treasury: For all they did cast in of their _____; but she of her want did cast in all that she had, even all her _____.

cast   living   treasury   abundance

13. Luke 3:11

He _____ and saith unto them, He that hath two _____, let him _____ to him that hath _____; and he that hath _____, let him do likewise.

meat   coats   impart   answereth   none

14. Luke 6:30

Give to every _____ that asketh of _____; and of him that taketh away thy _____ ask them not again.

thee   man   goods

15. Luke 6:38

    Give, and it shall be given unto you; good measure,
    pressed down, and _____ together, and _____
    over, shall men give into your _____. For with the
    same measure that ye mete withal it shall be _____ to
    you again.

    > measured shaken running bosom

16. Acts 20:35

    I have shewed you all _____, how that so _____
    ye ought to support the weak, and to remember the words
    of the Lord _____, how he said, It is more _____
    to give than to receive.

    > labouring blessed Jesus things

17. Romans 12:8

    Or he that exhorteth, on _____: he that giveth, let
    him do it with _____; he that ruleth, with _____;
    he that sheweth mercy, with _____.

    > diligence cheerfulness exhortation simplicity

18. 2 Corinthians 9:6–8

    But this I say, He which _____ sparingly shall reap
    also sparingly; and he which soweth bountifully shall reap
    also bountifully. Every man according as he purposeth
    in his _____, so let him give; not _____, or of
    necessity: for God loveth a cheerful giver. And God is able
    to make all grace _____ toward you; that ye, always
    having all _____ in all things, may abound to every
    good _____.

    > grudgingly heart soweth abound work sufficiency

19. 2 Corinthians 9:10

    Now he that ministereth _____ to the sower both
    minister _____ for your _____, and multiply
    your seed sown, and increase the _____ of your
    righteousness.

    fruits   seed   food   bread

20. Galatians 6:7

    Be not deceived; _____ is not _____: for
    whatsoever a man _____, that shall he also
    _____.

    reap   God   mocked   soweth

21. Philippians 4:15–17

    Now ye Philippians know also, that in the beginning of
    the _____, when I departed from Macedonia, no
    _____ communicated with me as concerning giving
    and receiving, but ye only. For even in Thessalonica ye
    sent once and again unto my _____. Not because I
    desire a gift: but I desire _____ that may _____
    to your _____.

    account   church   necessity   abound   fruit   gospel

22. James 2:15–16

    If a brother or _____ be naked, and destitute of daily
    _____, And one of you say unto them, Depart in
    peace, be ye warmed and _____; notwithstanding
    ye give them not those things which are needful to the
    _____; what doth it _____?

    filled   body   sister   food   profit

SPECIALIZED
MULTIPLE-CHOICE TRIVIA

Next is a large array of multiple-choice trivia by topic. Give yourself 1 point for each correct answer. Record your scores for each topic on the score card, and as always, you may repeat any or all of the quizzes as many times as necessary.

Take your time. This is not a race, and your ability to retain this information is greatly enhanced if you meditate on each answer.

All about Food

1. Who ate locusts in the wilderness?
   A. Matthew
   B. Paul
   C. John the Baptist
   D. Peter

2. Who traded his birthright for his brother's bread and lentil stew?
   A. Jacob
   B. David
   C. Joseph
   D. Esau

3. Who had a baker who baked pastries for him?
   A. The pharaoh in Moses's time
   B. The pharaoh in Joseph's time
   C. Samson
   D. Gideon

4. Who was tricked when his non-hairy son dressed in hairy gloves and presented him with a meal?
   A. Jacob
   B. Esau
   C. Isaac
   D. Israel

5. What did Ezekiel's scroll taste like?
   A. Candy
   B. Honey
   C. Fish
   D. Wafers

6. What judge of Israel prepared a delicious meal for an angel?
   A. Gideon
   B. Samson
   C. Ehud
   D. Deborah

7. What book of the Bible describes Canaan as a land flowing with milk and honey?
   A. Genesis
   B. Exodus
   C. Leviticus
   D. Judges

8. What animal was killed for food when the prodigal son returned home?
   A. A hog
   B. A rooster
   C. A turkey
   D. The fatted calf

9. Where did the Hebrews feast on cucumbers, melons, leeks, onions, and garlic?
   A. Jerusalem
   B. Bethlehem
   C. Egypt
   D. Gilead

10. Who ate honey out of a lion's carcass?
    A. David
    B. Elijah
    C. Saul
    D. Samson

11. What prophet made deadly stew edible again?
    A. Elijah
    B. Elisha
    C. Jeremiah
    D. Obadiah

12. What miraculous food fed the Israelites in the desert?
    A. Potatoes
    B. Manna
    C. Fish
    D. Five loaves of bread

13

From Sweet to Bitter

1. Who ate a book that was originally sweet but turned bitter?
   A. Peter
   B. Mark
   C. Thomas
   D. John

2. Who presented a riddle about finding something sweet in a lion's carcass?
   A. Elijah
   B. Elisha
   C. Samson
   D. Joel

3. According to Proverbs, what kind of bread is sweet to a man?
   A. Bread of deceit
   B. Bread of idleness
   C. Bread of comfort
   D. Bread of humbleness

4. What kind of grape sets the children's teeth on edge, according to Jeremiah?
   A. Red
   B. Green
   C. Sour
   D. Sweet

5. What type of herbs were the Israelites supposed to eat with the Passover meal?
   A. None
   B. Sweet herbs
   C. Bitter herbs
   D. Sour herbs

6. According to Proverbs, what kind of water is sweet?
   A. Purified water
   B. Rainwater
   C. River water
   D. Stolen water

7. What did Moses do to make the bitter waters of Marah drinkable?

A. He threw a piece of wood in the water.

B. He poured some honey in the water.

C. He prayed over the water.

D. He fasted several days.

8. After his resurrection, what did Jesus say his followers would be able to drink?

A. Juice

B. Milk

C. Water

D. Poison

9. What strange thing did Moses make the people of Israel drink?

A. Cane sugar

B. Honey

C. Silver

D. Gold dust

10. According to Proverbs, what sort of person thinks bitter things are sweet?

A. A conceited person

B. A prideful person

C. A hungry person

D. A loving person

Residential Area

1. What Genesis ship captain lived in a tent?
   A. Job
   B. Jonah
   C. Noah
   D. Nehemiah

2. Who stored Goliath's armor in his tent?
   A. Saul
   B. Jonathan
   C. Michal
   D. David

3. Who did Noah say would live in the tents of Shem?
   A. Japheth
   B. Ham
   C. Job
   D. Joel

4. Who took riches from Jericho and buried them in his tent?
   A. Amber
   B. Achan
   C. Uriah
   D. Aaron

5. Who took his wife to his mother's tent on their wedding night?
   A. Ishmael
   B. Isaac
   C. Jacob
   D. Esau

6. Who was "the father of such as dwell in tents"?
   A. Jabal
   B. Jacob
   C. Joseph
   D. Jonah

7. Who compared her dark skin to the darkness of the tents of Kedar?
   A. The woman in the Song of Solomon
   B. Eve
   C. Lydia
   D. The woman at the well

8. What prophet said, "The LORD also shall save the tents of Judah"?
   A. Nehemiah
   B. Jeremiah
   C. Zechariah
   D. Obadiah

9. Who murdered both an Israelite man and a Moabite woman inside a tent?
   A. Phinehas
   B. Naaman
   C. Jacob
   D. Abner

10. Who commanded his descendants to live in tents forever?
    A. David
    B. Jonadab
    C. Japheth
    D. Jabal

11. Who robbed the tents of the Syrians after the army fled their camp?
    A. The Samaritans
    B. The Jebusites
    C. The Levites
    D. The Benjamites

12. What prophet saw "the tents of Cushan in affliction"?
    A. Elijah
    B. Elisha
    C. Habakkuk
    D. Samuel

Kiddie Land

1. Who was the first child mentioned in the Bible?
   A. Cain
   B. Abel
   C. Seth
   D. Ham

2. Who was Noah's youngest son?
   A. Shem
   B. Japheth
   C. Ham
   D. Benjamin

3. What king was the youngest of eight brothers?
   A. Saul
   B. David
   C. Solomon
   D. Ahab

4. Who was the youngest son of Joseph?
   A. Manassah
   B. Ephraim
   C. Malachi
   D. Jair

5. Who of the following was not a son of Adam?
   A. Cain
   B. Abel
   C. Seth
   D. Ahab

6. Who died giving birth to Benjamin?
   A. Rebekah
   B. Rachel
   C. Rhoda
   D. Rahab

7. What judge had seventy sons?
   A. Samson
   B. Gideon
   C. Deborah
   D. Samuel

8. What king of Judah had twenty-eight sons and sixty daughters?
   A. Rehoboam
   B. David
   C. Solomon
   D. Saul

9. Who advised young Christians to stop thinking as children think?
   A. Peter
   B. Paul
   C. Pilate
   D. John

10. What king was severely distressed over the death of his wayward son?
    A. Saul
    B. Solomon
    C. David
    D. Heman

Did You Know?

(SET 3)

Prepare to be amazed by the following Bible facts.

- Approximately forty men wrote the Bible over a sixteen-hundred-year period. The time of the writing dates from 1500 BC to approximately AD 100.

- The Red Sea was not the only waterway parted by God. He also parted the Jordan River for Elijah and Elisha (2 Kings 2:7–9).

- Pontius Pilate and King Herod were bitter enemies until they became friends during Jesus's persecution (Luke 23:12).

- In the Gospels, Jesus is called the "Son of man" over seventy-five times.

- David kept Goliath's armor in his tent as a souvenir after slaying him (1 Samuel 17:54).

- Abraham was not circumcised until he was ninety-nine years old (Genesis 17:24).

- The place where Jesus was crucified, "the place of a skull," contained a garden (John 19:17–18, 41).

Window Display

1. Who died falling out of a window during one of Paul's sermons?
   A. Eutychus
   B. Esau
   C. Ephraim
   D. Naphtali

2. Who released two birds out of the window of a ship?
   A. Jacob
   B. Esau
   C. Noah
   D. David

3. Who was embarrassed when she looked out of her window and saw her husband dancing?
   A. Martha
   B. Michal
   C. Melissa
   D. Mary

4. Whose wife helped him escape the clutches of Saul via a window?
   A. David's
   B. Samuel's
   C. Uriah's
   D. Absalom's

5. What prophet commanded that a king shoot arrows out of a window?
   A. Elisha
   B. Elijah
   C. Ezra
   D. Ezekiel

6. Where did Paul escape a threat against his life by being let down by the wall in a basket?
   A. Damascus
   B. Corinth
   C. Ephesus
   D. Rome

7. What king peered out of his window and spotted Isaac and Rebekah being affectionate?
   A. David
   B. Saul
   C. Abimelech
   D. Solomon

8. What queen was hurled out of a window by her servants?
   A. Michal
   B. Rizpah
   C. Maachah
   D. Jezebel

9. Who saw a young man being approached by a prostitute while looking through his window?
   A. Solomon
   B. David
   C. Saul
   D. Absalom

10. What windows would be opened for people who tithed, according to the book of Malachi?
    A. Many blessings
    B. Windows of heaven
    C. Joyful windows
    D. Prayerful windows

18

That Makes Scents

1. What aromatic substance was brought to the baby Jesus?
   A. Ginger
   B. Frankincense
   C. Cinnamon
   D. Palm leaves

2. Whose harem contained women who were purified with various perfumes?
   A. King Herod
   B. King Ahaz
   C. King Josiah
   D. King Ahasuerus

3. In the Gospel of John, who anointed Jesus's feet with spikenard, an expensive ointment?
   A. Mary Magdalene
   B. Mary, mother of Jesus
   C. Mary, sister of Lazarus
   D. Mary, a nurse

4. In the Gospel of Luke, where was Jesus when a sinful woman poured an alabaster jar of perfume on his feet?
   A. At the home of Simon the Pharisee
   B. At Peter's house
   C. At the home of John and James
   D. In Bethlehem

5. What book of the Bible mentions a woman using spikenard, calamus, and various perfumes?
   A. Proverbs
   B. Psalms
   C. Song of Solomon
   D. Esther

6. Who perfumed her bed
   with myrrh, aloes, and
   cinnamon?
   A. The bride
   B. The harlot
   C. The mother
   D. The virtuous woman

7. What man used myrrh
   and frankincense as
   perfumes?
   A. Solomon
   B. David
   C. Saul
   D. Jonathan

8. What prophet refused
   to use anointing oils
   during mourning?
   A. Elijah
   B. Daniel
   C. Jonah
   D. Joel

9. According to the book
   of Proverbs, ointment
   and perfume do what?
   A. Help people to love
      everybody
   B. Rejoice the heart
   C. Make peace in the
      valley
   D. Bring laughter

10. What two prophets
    denounced women
    applying makeup?
    A. Elijah and Elisha
    B. Jonah and Joel
    C. Samuel and Josiah
    D. Jeremiah and
       Ezekiel

19

Nighty-Night

1. Who met a man who wrestled him all night?
   A. Jacob
   B. Jonah
   C. Jeremiah
   D. Joshua

2. Who passed through Egypt one night visiting nearly every household?
   A. Pharaoh
   B. The Lord
   C. Aaron
   D. Moses

3. Who paid a late-night visit to the young Samuel?
   A. Eli
   B. The Lord
   C. Moses
   D. Hannah

4. Who came to Peter in the dead of night and released him from prison?
   A. Rhoda
   B. The Lord
   C. An angel
   D. A guard

5. Who was visited by an angel who assured him he would be safe aboard a storm-ravaged ship?
   A. Jonah
   B. Peter
   C. Paul
   D. Judas

6. What Pharisee visited Jesus late at night?
   A. Cephas
   B. Gamaliel
   C. Paul
   D. Nicodemus

7. Who was mistakenly thought to be a spirit when spotted late one night?

A. An angel

B. Jesus

C. Paul

D. Peter

8. Who brought some officers of the chief priest to a late-night visit with Jesus?

A. Nicodemus

B. Philip

C. Peter

D. Judas

9. Who stole Saul's spear after creeping into his camp late one night?

A. Jonathan

B. David

C. Uriah

D. Samuel

10. Who visited a medium at night?

A. David

B. Samuel

C. Saul

D. Moses

11. Who attacked a Midianite camp late one night?

A. Joshua and his men

B. Gideon and his men

C. David and his men

D. Saul and his men

Wedding Bells

1. Who was the first man mentioned in the Bible to have more than one wife?
   A. Adam
   B. Lamech
   C. Moses
   D. Seth

2. Who married both Rachel and Leah?
   A. Lamech
   B. Abdon
   C. Jotham
   D. Jacob

3. Whose father's wives were named Hannah and Peninnah?
   A. Jacob's
   B. Samuel's
   C. Abraham's
   D. Isaac's

4. What king was married to Ahinoam?
   A. Josiah
   B. Saul
   C. David
   D. Solomon

5. Mahlon and Boaz were the husbands of what woman?
   A. Orpah
   B. Ruth
   C. Naomi
   D. Rachel

6. Who married two of Judah's sons?
   A. Rachel
   B. Leah
   C. Rebekah
   D. Tamar

7. What king of Judah had fourteen wives?
   A. Abijah
   B. Aaron
   C. Uzziah
   D. Saul

8. What judge of Israel surrendered his Philistine wife to a friend?
   A. Samson
   B. Othniel
   C. Ehud
   D. Gideon

Farming

1. Who planted the first garden?
   A. Adam
   B. Solomon
   C. Noah
   D. God

2. Who of the following was a farmer?
   A. Jacob
   B. Job
   C. Paul
   D. Stephen

3. What king planted many vineyards, gardens, and orchards?
   A. Pharaoh
   B. David
   C. Saul
   D. Solomon

4. What judge was also a farmer of grain?
   A. Gideon
   B. Othniel
   C. Deborah
   D. Joel

5. Who was the first man to plant a vineyard?
   A. Adam
   B. Cain
   C. Enoch
   D. Noah

6. What farmer and ancestor of David married a Moabite woman?
   A. Elimelech
   B. Ahaziah
   C. Boaz
   D. Ehud

7. Who was a farmer in Gerar and received a hundredfold harvest?
   A. Jacob
   B. Isaac
   C. Abraham
   D. Noah

8. What king of Judah enjoyed farming?
   A. Uzziah
   B. Ahaziah
   C. Amaziah
   D. Uriah

9. Who had a vineyard that was coveted by Ahab?
   A. Naaman
   B. Naboth
   C. Obadiah
   D. Omri

10. David commanded Ziba to farm for what lame man?
    A. Naaman
    B. Hezekiah
    C. Mephibosheth
    D. Jeroboam

SCRIPTURE
FILL IN THE BLANKS

Fill in the blanks to complete the following Scripture passages.
Give yourself 2 points for each correct passage.

Fill in the Blanks

1. Genesis 1:1
   In the _____ God created the _____ and the
   _____.

2. Psalm 37:4
   Delight _____ also in the _____: and he shall
   give thee the _____ of thine _____.

3. Isaiah 9:6
   For unto us a _____ is born, unto us a son is given:
   and the _____ shall be upon his shoulder: and his
   name shall be called _____, Counsellor, The mighty
   God, The everlasting Father, The Prince of _____.

4. Isaiah 40:28
   Hast thou not _____? hast thou not heard, that the
   _____ God, the LORD, the Creator of the ends of
   the earth, fainteth not, neither is _____? there is no
   searching of his understanding.

5. Jeremiah 29:11
   For I know the _____ that I think toward you, saith
   the _____, thoughts of peace, and not of _____,
   to give you an expected end.

6. John 3:16
   For God so _____ the _____, that he gave his
   only begotten _____, that whosoever believeth in
   him should not perish, but have everlasting _____.

7. John 15:7

   If ye _____ in me, and my words abide in you, ye shall ask what ye _____, and it shall be done unto _____.

8. Romans 4:21

   And being _____ persuaded that, what he had _____, he was able also to _____.

9. Romans 8:1

   There is therefore now no _____ to them which are in Christ _____, who walk not after the flesh, but after the _____.

10. Romans 8:28

    And we know that all things _____ together for _____ to them that _____ God, to them who are the called according to his _____.

11. 2 Corinthians 1:20

    For all the _____ of God in him are yea, and in him _____, unto the _____ of God by us.

12. Ephesians 2:10

    For we are his workmanship, created in Christ Jesus unto good _____, which God hath before _____ that we should walk in them.

13. Philippians 4:6–7

    Be careful for _____; but in every thing by _____ and supplication with _____ let your requests be made known unto God. And the peace of God, which passeth all understanding, shall keep your hearts and _____ through Christ Jesus.

14. Philippians 4:19

     But my God shall _____ all your need according to
     his _____ in _____ by Christ Jesus.

15. 2 Peter 1:4

     Whereby are given unto us exceeding _____ and
     precious _____: that by these ye might be partakers
     of the divine _____, having escaped the corruption
     that is in the world through lust.

Scriptures on Salvation

1. John 14:6
   Jesus saith unto him, I am the _____, the truth, and
   the _____: no man cometh unto the _____, but
   by me.

2. Romans 3:23
   For all have _____, and come short of the _____
   of God.

3. Romans 6:23
   For the wages of _____ is _____; but the gift of
   God is eternal _____ through Jesus Christ our Lord.

4. 2 Corinthians 5:17
   Therefore if any man be in _____, he is a new
   _____: old things are passed away; behold, all things
   are become _____.

5. Ephesians 2:8–9
   For by _____ are ye saved through _____; and
   that not of yourselves: it is the gift of God: Not of works,
   lest any man should _____.

6. Revelation 3:20
   Behold, I stand at the _____, and _____: if any
   man hear my _____, and open the door, I will come
   in to him, and will sup with him, and he with me.

Scriptures on Security

1. Psalm 27:1
   The _____ is my light and my _____; whom shall I fear? the LORD is the strength of my life; of whom shall I be _____?

2. Psalm 37:4
   Delight _____ also in the LORD: and he shall give thee the _____ of thine _____.

3. Proverbs 3:5–6
   Trust in the _____ with all thine heart; and lean not unto thine own _____. In all thy ways acknowledge him, and he shall direct thy _____.

4. Isaiah 40:31
   But they that _____ upon the _____ shall renew their strength; they shall mount up with wings as eagles; they shall run, and not be _____; and they shall walk, and not _____.

5. Jeremiah 29:11
   For I know the thoughts that I think toward you, saith the _____, thoughts of _____, and not of _____, to give you an expected end.

6. Lamentations 3:22–23

   It is of the LORD's _____ that we are not _____, because his compassions fail not. They are new every morning: great is thy _____.

7. Matthew 11:28–30

   Come unto me, all ye that labour and are heavy _____, and I will give you rest. Take my _____ upon you, and learn of me; for I am meek and lowly in _____: and ye shall find rest unto your souls. For my yoke is easy, and my burden is _____.

8. Luke 16:13

   No _____ can serve two _____: for either he will hate the one, and love the other; or else he will hold to the one, and despise the other. Ye cannot serve _____ and mammon.

9. Acts 1:8

   But ye shall receive _____, after that the Holy _____ is come upon you: and ye shall be witnesses unto me both in _____, and in all Judaea, and in Samaria, and unto the uttermost part of the _____.

10. Romans 8:28

    And we know that all _____ work together for _____ to them that love God, to them who are the called according to his _____.

11. Romans 8:38–39

    For I am persuaded, that neither _____, nor life, nor _____, nor principalities, nor powers, nor things present, nor things to come, Nor _____, nor depth, nor any other creature, shall be able to separate us from the love of God, which is in Christ Jesus our _____.

12. Romans 12:1

    I beseech you therefore, _____, by the mercies
    of _____, that ye present your bodies a living
    _____, holy, acceptable unto God, which is your
    reasonable _____.

13. 1 Corinthians 15:58

    Therefore, my beloved brethren, be ye stedfast,
    _____, always abounding in the _____ of the
    Lord, forasmuch as ye know that your labour is not in
    _____ in the Lord.

14. 2 Corinthians 4:18

    While we _____ not at the things which are
    _____, but at the things which are not seen: for the
    things which are seen are _____; but the things which
    are not seen are _____.

15. 2 Corinthians 12:9

    And he said unto me, My _____ is sufficient for
    _____: for my strength is made perfect in weakness.
    Most gladly therefore will I rather glory in my _____,
    that the power of Christ may rest upon me.

16. Galatians 2:20

    I am _____ with Christ: nevertheless I live; yet not I,
    but Christ liveth in me: and the _____ which I now
    live in the flesh I live by the _____ of the Son of God,
    who loved me, and gave himself for me.

17. Galatians 5:22–23

    But the _____ of the Spirit is love, joy, peace,
    _____, gentleness, goodness, _____, Meekness,
    temperance: against such there is no law.

18. Philippians 4:13
    I can do all _____ through Christ which _____ me.

19. Colossians 3:23
    And whatsoever ye do, do it _____, as to the Lord,
    and not unto _____.

20. Hebrews 12:1–2
    Wherefore seeing we also are compassed about with
    so great a cloud of _____, let us lay aside every
    _____, and the sin which doth so easily beset us,
    and let us run with patience the race that is set before
    us, looking unto Jesus the author and finisher of our
    _____; who for the joy that was set before him
    endured the _____, despising the shame, and is set
    down at the right hand of the throne of God.

21. Hebrews 13:8
    Jesus Christ the same _____, and to day, and for
    _____.

22. James 1:22
    But be ye _____ of the _____, and not hearers
    only, deceiving your own _____.

23. James 4:7
    _____ yourselves therefore to _____. Resist the
    devil, and he will _____ from you.

24. 2 Peter 3:9
    The _____ is not slack concerning his _____,
    as some men count slackness; but is longsuffering to us-
    ward, not willing that any should _____, but that all
    should come to repentance.

25. 1 John 4:7–8

    Beloved, let us _____ one another: for love is of God; and every one that loveth is born of God, and knoweth _____. He that loveth not knoweth not God; for God is love.

Crossword Puzzle 1

Tackle this first of two crossword puzzles for 25 bonus points. Since crossword puzzles are difficult by nature, you are allowed three mistakes without penalty. If you solve the puzzle with only three mistakes or fewer, give yourself 25 points in the bonus column of the score card.

Across

2. Caspar, Balthazar, and Melchior
4. Christian symbol
6. First gardener
7. Apostle to the Gentiles
8. Proverbs 19:15, Slothfulness casteth into a deep sleep; and an ___ soul shall suffer hunger
11. Chief heavenly messenger, like Gabriel
13. Daniel 7:1, In the first year of Belshazzar king of Babylon Daniel had a dream and visions of his head upon his ___
14. A gift to the infant Jesus
17. Certain man of the cloth
18. Psalm 106:16, They envied Moses also in the camp, and Aaron the ___ of the LORD
19. Adore to the fullest
22. Genesis 7:22, ___ whose nostrils was the breath of life, of all that was in the dry land, died (2 words)
23. Confidence that God's Word is true
25. Period beginning Ash Wednesday
26. Church building feature
27. Mother of Abel
28. The wages of it are death

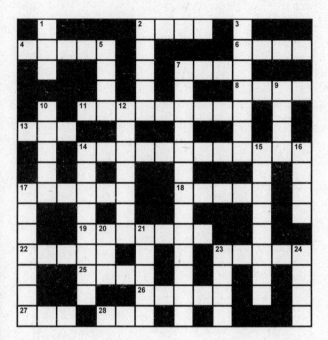

Down

1. How great thou ___
2. Proverbs 7:17, I have perfumed my bed with ___, aloes, and cinnamon
3. Nazareth's locale
5. Revelation 8:11, And the name of the ___ is called Wormwood
7. He ordered Christ's crucifixion
9. The Ten Commandments, for example
10. Man originally called Simon
12. Thing with verses in the Bible
14. What God has given so that people can make their own choices (2 words)
15. Christmas scene
16. Twin in Genesis
17. Kind of story Jesus told
20. Genesis 11:1, And the whole earth was of ___ language
21. The enemy to us all
23. Genesis 19:24, Then the LORD rained upon Sodom and upon Gomorrah brimstone and ___
24. Psalm 9:17, The wicked shall be turned into ___, and all the nations that forget God

SECTION 2

THE ADVANCED SECTION

This section gets into very specific and challenging questions and puzzles geared to take you to an extreme level of Bible brilliance. (Answers to section 2 begin on page 240).

> If we abide by the principles taught in the Bible, our country will go on prospering but if we and our posterity neglect its instructions and authority, no man can tell how sudden a catastrophe may overwhelm us and bury all our glory in profound obscurity.
>
> Daniel Webster, American statesman and the fourteenth United States secretary of state

SPECIALIZED
TRUE OR FALSE TRIVIA

For 1 point per correct answer, tackle this section of true or false statements derived from all areas of the Bible. Some are easy, and some are quite difficult. Do one group at a time and record your score for each group on the score card.

Remember, you may do a single group as many times as necessary before posting your best score. It is far more important to be thorough and to learn this information than to finish quickly and retain little.

Group 1

1. _____ Isaac was the son of Abraham.

2. _____ Matthew was David's firstborn son.

3. _____ Solomon's son Shaphat became king after him.

4. _____ The apostle Paul said that a woman's long hair is her pride and joy.

5. _____ Flesh and blood is unable to inherit the kingdom of God.

6. _____ In the Bible, sin is called the sting of death.

7. _____ All believers are called to be the temple of God, according to Paul.

8. _____ Paul refers to himself as a missionary in the book of 1 Corinthians.

9. _____ David promised Bathsheba that her son Solomon would one day be governor.

10. _____ Rehoboam ruled in Judah for twenty-one years.

11. _____ King Ahab was the husband of Jezebel.

12. _____ In Samaria, Ahab built a temple for Baal.

13. _____ Elisha brought a widow's son back from the dead in Zarephath.

14. _____ Ravens brought Elijah food in a dire situation.

15. _____ On Mount Nebo, Elijah met the prophets of Baal.

16. _____ Elijah once outran a king's chariot to the town of Jezreel.

17. _____ The prophet Elijah was fed three meals by an angel.

18. _____ When Elijah fled from Jezebel, he went to Mount Horeb.

19. _____ Mount Horeb is called the mount of God.

20. _____ King Solomon had twelve thousand horsemen.

Group 2

1. _____ Abner was the commander of Solomon's army.

2. _____ David received permission from the Lord to build the temple.

3. _____ In Solomon's first year as king, he began to build the house of the Lord.

4. _____ Jesus is the chief corner stone.

5. _____ The apostle Peter compared the devil to a roaring lion.

6. _____ Hannah received a son after asking God to bless her with a child.

7. _____ The first king of Israel was Saul.

8. _____ A person's hand was the part of the body that was usually anointed.

9. _____ Because King Saul acted as a priest in Samuel's place, he was rejected.

10. _____ David's father was Jesse.

11. _____ David had a skill for playing the harp.

12. _____ David boasted of killing a pig and a horse.

13. _____ Bartimaeus was healed of blindness.

14. _____ The gigantic Goliath was from the city of Ekron.

15. _____ Goliath stood over nine feet tall (six cubits and a span).

16. _____ David took seven stones from the brook before killing Goliath.

17. _____ To bring down Goliath, David used a huge sword.

18. _____ David stored Goliath's armor in his tent.

19. _____ Saul once threw a javelin at David.

20. _____ David's first wife was Michal.

Group 3

1. _____ The women of Israel danced when Goliath was killed by David.

2. _____ Hannah made a robe every year for her son.

3. _____ In 1 Samuel, Jonathan and David made a covenant of friendship.

4. _____ The priest of Nod gave Saul's sword to David.

5. _____ Saul massacred eighty-five priests in the town of Nazareth.

6. _____ David's wife Abigail was also married to a man named Nabal.

7. _____ At night, Saul visited a medium.

8. _____ When Samuel was a boy, he was awakened out of his sleep by the voice of God.

9. _____ Saul's bones were buried under a bridge at Jabesh.

10. _____ Saul's sons were killed by the Philistines.

11. _____ King Saul was critically wounded by Philistine arrows.

12. _____ Six of Saul's sons were killed in battle.

13. _____ Eli's sons were killed when the ark was taken.

14. _____ The ark of the covenant was taken into battle with the Philistines by Eli's sons.

15. _____ Dagon was the god of the Philistines.

16. _____ Samuel, a judge and a prophet, built an altar to the Lord at Ramah.

17. _____ Samuel's home was in the city of Ramah.

18. _____ Kish was the father of King Saul.

19. _____ Jesus Christ is the mediator between God and man.

20. _____ Paul told Timothy that Christians should lift up a symbol of the cross in prayer.

Group 4

1. _____ Abijah, king of Judah, had fourteen wives.

2. _____ The Philistines brought a tribute to King Jehoshaphat.

3. _____ In a vision, the prophet Micaiah saw the Lord sitting upon a mountain.

4. _____ Solomon got the cedars for his temple from Lebanon.

5. _____ King Uzziah dug wells in the desert.

6. _____ Uzziah, the king of Judah, was a leper until he died.

7. _____ Moses disguised himself before fighting with an Egyptian.

8. _____ Paul's nationality was Greek.

9. _____ Paul suffered shipwrecks three times.

10. _____ Eve's name appears seven times in the New Testament.

11. _____ The apostle Paul fled from the soldiers of King Aretas in Damascus.

12. _____ Paul knew of a man who had been caught up into the third heaven.

13. _____ The bones of Elisha healed a man of leprosy.

14. _____ Elijah was taken to heaven in a whirlwind.

15. _____ When Elisha struck the Jordan River with Elijah's cloak, it turned red.

16. _____ Elisha was used by God to heal the waters of Gibeah with a bowl of salt.

17. _____ Hezekiah and Joshua had time altered for them.

18. _____ Josiah was only eight years old when he became king, and he reigned in Jerusalem thirty-one years.

19. _____ King Josiah was killed in Megiddo.

20. _____ Nebuchadnezzar was a ruler of Babylon.

Group 5

1. _____ David was the last king of Judah.

2. _____ Elisha's servant was Gehazi.

3. _____ Elisha supplied a widow with large quantities of milk and honey.

4. _____ For lying to the prophet Elisha, Gehazi was turned into a leper.

5. _____ Elisha's servant had a vision of the hills filled with horses and chariots of fire.

6. _____ Hazael murdered King Benhadad.

7. _____ The prophet Urijah was murdered for opposing King Jehoiakim.

8. _____ King Jehu ordered Jezebel's servants to toss her out the window.

9. _____ After Jezebel's death, wild horses ate her body.

10. _____ David saw his neighbor bathing on a rooftop.

11. _____ Nathan, a prophet, confronted King David about his sin of adultery.

12. _____ Absalom was David and Bathsheba's second son.

13. _____ God named Solomon Jedidiah.

14. _____ After killing his brother Amnon, Absalom fled to Geshur for three years.

15. _____ David's son Absalom was known for being an unattractive man.

16. _____ As David went up the Mount of Olives, he was barefoot and wept.

17. _____ Absalom was buried by Joab in a great pit in the forest.

18. _____ David was anointed king at Hebron.

19. _____ Saul's son Ishbosheth was made king over Israel by Abner.

20. _____ King Saul's son Ishbosheth was also known as Titus.

Group 6

1. _____ The wise woman of Abel saved her city by negotiating with Joab.

2. _____ Joab killed a man while kissing him.

3. _____ David moved the bones of Saul and his son Jonathan to their final place of burial.

4. _____ Saul's grandson Mephibosheth was crippled in both feet.

5. _____ While pretending to get wheat, Rechab and Baanah killed a king.

6. _____ Amorites inhabited Jerusalem before the Israelites.

7. _____ In her heart, Michal despised her husband, David.

8. _____ Jehu was the commander of David's army.

9. _____ Timothy's grandmother's name was Hilda.

10. _____ Lydia was Timothy's mother.

11. _____ Paul sent Tychicus to Ephesus.

12. _____ Four soldiers were stationed with Peter in his cell.

13. _____ Matthias succeeded Judas Iscariot as an apostle.

14. _____ Peter led a Roman soldier named Cornelius to Christ.

15. _____ Cornelius was baptized by Peter.

16. _____ Believers were first called Christians at the church in Thessalonica.

17. _____ Agabus prophesied there would be a famine in the land.

18. _____ Philip was the first apostle to be martyred.

19. _____ The first apostle to be martyred was James.

20. _____ Herod ordered the jail keepers be put to death after Peter escaped.

Group 7

1. _____ Herod was eaten by worms before he died.

2. _____ Peter was released from prison by an angel.

3. _____ Barnabas and Paul were deserted by Mark in Perga.

4. _____ The apostle Paul was originally known as Saul.

5. _____ Paul was stoned in the city of Lystra.

6. _____ Silas, Paul's traveling companion, was considered a prophet.

7. _____ On Paul's second missionary journey, he was accompanied by John the Baptist.

8. _____ Lydia was a seller of purple cloth.

9. _____ The Lord opened Lydia's heart to respond to Paul's message.

10. _____ Lydia was baptized by Paul and Silas.

11. _____ The Bereans were famous for writing gospel songs.

12. _____ Claudius demanded all the Jews depart from Rome.

13. _____ Crispus, a synagogue leader, was a member of the church in Corinth.

14. _____ The church in Ephesus was the scene of a burning of wicked books.

15. _____ The school of Tyrannus was in Corinth.

16. _____ John preached at Pentecost.

17. _____ Eutychus was in Assos when he fell out of a window.

18. _____ Both Paul and Peter raised people from the dead.

19. _____ Paul's hometown was Tarsus in Cilicia.

20. _____ Paul's teacher was a famous rabbi named Gamaliel.

Group 8

1. _____ Paul studied under Gamaliel.

2. _____ Paul's nephew came to sing Paul songs while he was imprisoned in Jerusalem.

3. _____ Forty men made an oath to fast until they had killed Paul.

4. _____ Tertullus prosecuted Paul when he was in Caesarea.

5. _____ Festus replaced Felix as governor of Judea.

6. _____ Felix, wanting to do a favor for the Jews, let Paul out of prison.

7. _____ Euroclydon was the name of a false god.

8. _____ Paul was not affected when a viper bit him.

9. _____ James healed a crippled man at the Beautiful Gate.

10. _____ Barnabas means "the son of consolation."

11. _____ Barnabas means "the son of peace."

12. _____ Bartholomew was Barnabas's original name.

13. _____ About six thousand men accepted Christ when Peter spoke on the day of Pentecost.

14. _____ A Pharisee was considered a servant.

15. _____ Gamaliel was described as a teacher of the law.

16. _____ Stephen was the first Christian to be martyred.

17. _____ Stephen was stoned to death.

18. _____ An angel carried Philip from Gaza to Azotus.

19. _____ King David tried to buy the gifts of the Holy Spirit.

20. _____ Peter was headed to Damascus to arrest Christians.

Group 9

1. _____ Aeneas was healed from palsy by John the Baptist.

2. _____ John the Baptist raised Dorcas from the dead.

3. _____ After the apostle Paul saw a vision of Jesus, he temporarily lost his sight.

4. _____ Before Amos was a prophet, he was a carpenter.

5. _____ Amos spoke about justice rolling down like a boulder.

6. _____ Paul told believers to set their affections on things around them.

7. _____ Paul described his friend Luke as a beloved brother.

8. _____ Nebuchadnezzar was king of Egypt.

9. _____ Before the Babylonians changed Meshach's Jewish name, it was Daniel.

10. _____ Nebuchadnezzar had worrisome dreams that kept him from sleeping.

11. _____ Nebuchadnezzar promised various gifts, rewards, and great honor to the person who could interpret his dream.

12. _____ During Belshazzar's feast, a mysterious hand wrote on the wall.

13. _____ David was the only king in the Bible referred to as "the Mede."

14. _____ King Darius ordered Daniel be thrown into the lions' den.

15. _____ Daniel would kneel and pray five times a day.

16. _____ King Darius fasted after Daniel was thrown into the lions' den.

17. _____ Daniel had a vision of a horse with eagle's wings.

18. _____ The angel Gabriel gave Daniel an understanding of the future.

19. _____ The angel Gabriel visited David while he was confessing his sins.

20. _____ When Moses died, he was 130 years old.

Group 10

1. _____ Eleazar succeeded his father, Aaron, as priest.

2. _____ The Israelites were commanded to bring firstborn animals to God for sacrifice.

3. _____ Og, the king of Bashan, had a bed made of iron.

4. _____ On the mountain of Nebo, Moses was given a view into the Promised Land.

5. _____ During the time of Moses, the city of Jericho was also known as the city of palm trees.

6. _____ God buried Moses in the land of Moab.

7. _____ The Israelites mourned Moses for seventy days.

8. _____ The Lord tells us to honor our mother and father.

9. _____ God described the Israelites as being stiffnecked.

10. _____ The book of Ecclesiastes says laughter is madness (NKJV).

11. _____ In Ephesians, sleepers are told to rise from the dead.

12. _____ Paul recommended the Holy Spirit as a substitute for food.

13. _____ Adah was Esther's Hebrew name.

14. _____ Esther was an orphan.

15. _____ Haman was angry with Mordecai because he stole his cattle.

16. _____ Haman planned to destroy all of the Jews.

17. _____ Tamar was the wife of Haman of Persia.

18. _____ The Egyptians made the Israelites into slaves.

19. _____ Pharaoh made a false confession to Moses and Aaron.

20. _____ God blew a strong west wind and stopped the locust plague.

36

Did You Know?

(SET 4)

Here are more wonderful mind benders from the Bible.

- Three squared is nine. Those two digits are thirty-nine. There are thirty-nine books in the Old Testament. Three times nine equals twenty-seven. There are twenty-seven books in the New Testament.

- Moses did not cast down the rod that transformed into a snake before Pharaoh. It was his brother, Aaron (Exodus 7:8–12).

- Second Samuel 12:1–14 tells of the prophet Nathan confronting David with a parable about David's sinful, adulterous affair with Bathsheba and her husband's murder. David became angry after hearing the parable and said the sinful man featured in it should die and make a fourfold restitution. Since the sinful man of the parable was David himself, David's "judgment" for the man in the parable came true. David killed one man, Bathsheba's husband, but four of David's sons died, a fourfold restitution (2 Samuel 12:15–19; 13:28–33; 18:14–15; 1 Kings 2:23–25).

- Samson once caught three hundred foxes and tied them tail to tail. Between the knotted tails, Samson inserted lit torches and released the frantic foxes to burn up the fields of the Philistines (Judges 15:4–5).

- In the book of Joshua, there is a woman named Noah (Joshua 17:3).

37

Memory Verses

Every brilliant Bible scholar has memorized a good portion of Scripture. I have carefully selected some of the most important passages in the Bible for the next step in becoming Bible brilliant. In the following exercise, fill in the blanks using the words listed below each Scripture passage. Give yourself 2 points for each passage you complete accurately.

1. Genesis 1:1
   In the _____ God created the _____ and the
   _____.

   earth   heaven   beginning

2. Genesis 1:26
   And God said, Let us make man in our _____, after our likeness: and let them have _____ over the fish of the sea, and over the fowl of the air, and over the cattle, and over all the earth, and over every creeping thing that creepeth upon the _____.

   image   dominion   earth

3. Genesis 1:27
   So God created man in his own _____, in the image of God created he him; _____ and _____ created he them.

   female   image   male

4. Joshua 1:8

   This book of the law shall not depart out of thy _____;
   but thou shalt meditate therein day and _____, that
   thou mayest observe to do according to all that is written
   therein: for then thou shalt make thy way _____, and
   then thou shalt have good _____.

   > prosperous   success   night   mouth

5. Joshua 1:9

   Have not I commanded thee? Be strong and of a good
   _____; be not afraid, neither be thou _____: for
   the LORD thy God is with _____ whithersoever thou
   goest.

   > dismayed   thee   courage

6. Psalm 37:4

   Delight _____ also in the LORD; and he shall give
   thee the _____ of thine _____.

   > desires   heart   thyself

7. Psalm 133:1–2

   Behold, how good and how pleasant it is for _____
   to dwell together in _____! It is like the precious
   _____ upon the head, that ran down upon the
   _____, even Aaron's beard: that went down to the
   skirts of his garments.

   > beard   ointment   brethren   unity

8. Psalm 139:14

   I will praise thee; for I am _____ and _____
   made: marvellous are thy _____; and that my soul
   knoweth right well.

   > wonderfully   works   fearfully

9. Proverbs 3:5–6

_____ in the LORD with all thine _____; and
lean not unto thine own understanding. In all thy ways
_____ him, and he shall direct thy _____.

> acknowledge   trust   paths   heart

10. Proverbs 30:5

Every _____ of _____ is pure: he is a shield unto
them that put their _____ in him.

> God   word   trust

11. Isaiah 26:3

Thou wilt keep him in perfect _____, whose
_____ is stayed on thee: because he _____ in
thee.

> trusteth   peace   mind

12. Isaiah 40:31

But they that wait upon the LORD shall renew their
_____; they shall mount up with _____ as
_____; they shall run, and not be weary; and they
shall walk, and not _____.

> eagles   strength   faint   wings

13. Isaiah 41:10

Fear thou not; for I am with thee: be not _____; for
I am thy God: I will strengthen thee; yea, I will help thee;
yea, I will uphold _____ with the right _____ of
my righteousness.

> hand   dismayed   thee

14. Isaiah 53:4

    Surely he hath borne our _____, and carried our
    sorrows: yet we did esteem him _____, smitten of
    God, and _____.

    afflicted   griefs   stricken

15. Isaiah 53:5

    But he was wounded for our _____, he was bruised
    for our _____: the _____ of our peace was upon
    him; and with his _____ we are healed.

    chastisement   stripes   transgressions   iniquities

16. Isaiah 53:6

    All we like _____ have gone _____; we have
    turned every one to his own way; and the LORD hath laid
    on him the _____ of us all.

    iniquity   astray   sheep

17. Isaiah 55:8

    For my thoughts are not your _____, neither are your
    ways my _____, saith the _____.

    LORD   thoughts   ways

18. Jeremiah 29:11

    For I know the thoughts that I think toward you, saith the
    LORD, thoughts of _____, and not of _____, to
    give you an expected _____.

    evil   peace   end

19. Micah 6:8

    He hath shewed _____, O man, what is good; and
    what doth the _____ require of thee, but to do justly,
    and to love _____, and to walk _____ with thy
    God?

    mercy   humbly   thee   LORD

20. Matthew 3:2
    And saying, _____ ye: for the _____ of heaven is
    at _____.

    hand   kingdom   repent

21. Matthew 5:16
    Let your _____ so shine before men, that they may
    see your _____ works, and glorify your Father which
    is in _____.

    good   light   heaven

22. Matthew 11:28–30
    Come unto me, all ye that labour and are heavy laden,
    and I will give you _____. Take my _____ upon
    you, and learn of me; for I am _____ and lowly in
    _____: and ye shall find rest unto your souls. For my
    yoke is easy, and my burden is light.

    yoke   rest   heart   meek

23. Matthew 22:37
    _____ said unto him, Thou shalt _____ the Lord
    thy God with all thy heart, and with all thy _____,
    and with all thy _____.

    mind   love   Jesus   soul

24. Matthew 28:18
    And _____ came and spake unto them, saying,
    All _____ is given unto me in _____ and in
    _____.

    heaven   Jesus   earth   power

25. Matthew 28:19–20

    Go ye therefore, and teach all _____, baptizing them
    in the name of the Father, and of the Son, and of the
    Holy _____: Teaching them to _____ all things
    whatsoever I have _____ you: and, lo, I am with you
    always, even unto the end of the world. Amen.

    commanded   observe   nations   Ghost

26. John 1:1

    In the _____ was the _____, and the Word was
    with God, and the Word was _____.

    Word   beginning   God

27. John 1:12

    But as many as received him, to them gave he _____
    to become the sons of God, even to them that _____
    on his _____.

    name   power   believe

28. John 3:16

    For God so loved the _____, that he gave his only
    begotten Son, that whosoever believeth in him should not
    _____, but have everlasting _____.

    perish   life   world

29. John 3:17

    For God sent not his Son into the _____ to
    _____ the world; but that the world through him
    might be _____.

    saved   condemn   world

30. John 5:24

Verily, verily, I say unto you, He that heareth my
_____, and believeth on him that sent me,
hath everlasting _____, and shall not come into
condemnation; but is passed from _____ unto life.

death   word   life

31. John 10:10

The _____ cometh not, but for to steal, and to
_____, and to _____: I am come that they
might have _____, and that they might have it more
abundantly.

life   destroy   kill   thief

32. John 11:25

Jesus said unto her, I am the _____, and the life: he
that believeth in me, though he were _____, yet shall
he _____.

dead   resurrection   live

33. John 13:35

By this shall all _____ know that ye are my
_____, if ye have _____ one to another.

disciples   men   love

34. John 14:6

_____ saith unto him, I am the way, the _____,
and the _____: no man cometh unto the _____,
but by me.

Father   truth   life   Jesus

35. John 14:27

    Peace I leave with you, my _____ I give unto you:
    not as the _____ giveth, give I unto you. Let not your
    _____ be troubled, neither let it be afraid.

    peace   world   heart

36. John 15:13

    Greater _____ hath no _____ than this, that a
    man lay down his _____ for his _____.

    life   love   friends   man

37. John 16:33

    These things I have spoken unto you, that in me ye
    might have _____. In the _____ ye shall have
    _____: but be of good _____; I have overcome
    the world.

    tribulation   peace   world   cheer

38. Acts 1:8

    But ye shall receive _____, after that the Holy Ghost
    is come upon you: and ye shall be _____ unto me
    both in _____, and in all Judaea, and in _____,
    and unto the uttermost part of the _____.

    Samaria   power   earth   Jerusalem   witnesses

39. Acts 2:38

    Then _____ said unto them, Repent, and be
    _____ every one of you in the name of Jesus Christ
    for the remission of _____, and ye shall receive the
    _____ of the Holy Ghost.

    sins   baptized   Peter   gift

40. Acts 4:12

    Neither is there _____ in any other: for there is none
    other _____ under heaven given among _____,
    whereby we must be _____.

    men   saved   name   salvation

41. Acts 17:11

    These were more noble than those in _____, in that
    they received the word with all readiness of _____, and
    searched the _____ daily, whether those _____
    were so.

    things   Thessalonica   mind   scriptures

42. Romans 3:23

    For all have _____, and come short of the _____
    of _____.

    glory   sinned   God

43. Romans 5:8

    But _____ commendeth his _____ toward us, in
    that, while we were yet sinners, _____ died for us.

    Christ   love   God

44. Romans 6:23

    For the wages of _____ is _____; but the gift of
    God is eternal life through Jesus Christ our _____.

    Lord   sin   death

45. Romans 8:28

    And we know that all things _____ together for good
    to them that love _____, to them who are the called
    according to his _____.

    purpose   work   God

46. Romans 8:38–39

    For I am persuaded, that neither _____, nor life,
    nor angels, nor principalities, nor _____, nor things
    present, nor things to come, Nor height, nor depth, nor
    any other _____, shall be able to separate us from the
    love of God, which is in Christ Jesus our _____.

    creature   death   powers   Lord

47. Romans 10:9–10

    That if thou shalt confess with thy _____ the Lord
    Jesus, and shalt believe in thine _____ that God hath
    raised him from the _____, thou shalt be saved. For
    with the heart man believeth unto righteousness; and
    with the mouth confession is made unto _____.

    heart   salvation   mouth   dead

48. Romans 10:17

    So then _____ cometh by _____, and hearing by
    the _____ of God.

    hearing   word   faith

49. Romans 12:1

    I beseech you therefore, brethren, by the _____ of
    God, that ye present your _____ a living _____,
    holy, acceptable unto _____, which is your reasonable
    service.

    sacrifice   God   mercies   bodies

50. Romans 12:2

    And be not _____ to this world: but be ye
    transformed by the renewing of your _____, that ye
    may prove what is that good, and _____, and perfect,
    _____ of God.

    acceptable   conformed   mind   will

51. Romans 15:13

Now the God of _____ fill you with all joy and
_____ in believing, that ye may abound in hope,
through the _____ of the Holy Ghost.

hope   peace   power

52. 1 Corinthians 6:19

What? know ye not that your _____ is the temple of
the _____ _____ which is in you, which ye have
of God, and ye are not your own?

Ghost   body   Holy

53. 1 Corinthians 10:13

There hath no temptation taken you but such as is
common to man: but God is _____, who will not
_____ you to be tempted above that ye are able; but
will with the _____ also make a way to _____,
that ye may be able to bear it.

faithful   temptation   escape   suffer

54. 2 Corinthians 5:17

Therefore if any _____ be in Christ, he is a new
_____: old _____ are passed away; behold, all
things are become new.

creature   man   things

55. 2 Corinthians 5:21

For he hath made him to be sin for us, who knew no
_____; that we might be made the _____ of God
in _____.

righteousness   him   sin

56. 2 Corinthians 12:9
    And he said unto me, My _____ is sufficient for thee:
    for my _____ is made perfect in _____. Most gladly
    therefore will I rather glory in my _____, that the
    power of Christ may rest upon me.

    infirmities   weakness   grace   strength

57. 2 Timothy 1:7
    For God hath not given us the _____ of _____;
    but of _____, and of love, and of a sound _____.

    power   mind   spirit   fear

58. 2 Timothy 3:16–17
    All _____ is given by inspiration of God, and is
    profitable for _____, for reproof, for correction, for
    _____ in righteousness: That the man of God may be
    perfect, thoroughly furnished unto all good _____.

    works   doctrine   scripture   instruction

59. Hebrews 4:12
    For the word of God is quick, and powerful, and sharper
    than any twoedged sword, piercing even to the dividing
    asunder of _____ and _____, and of the joints
    and _____, and is a discerner of the thoughts and
    intents of the _____.

    marrow   spirit   heart   soul

60. Hebrews 4:15
    For we have not an high priest which cannot be
    _____ with the feeling of our _____; but was in
    all points _____ like as we are, yet without sin.

    infirmities   touched   tempted

61. Hebrews 4:16

Let us therefore come _____ unto the throne of _____, that we may obtain _____, and find grace to _____ in time of need.

> boldly   mercy   help   grace

62. Hebrews 10:24–25

And let us consider one _____ to provoke unto _____ and to good _____: Not forsaking the _____ of ourselves together, as the manner of some is; but exhorting one another: and so much the more, as ye see the day approaching.

> another   assembling   works   love

63. Hebrews 11:1

Now _____ is the _____ of things hoped for, the _____ of things not seen.

> substance   faith   evidence

64. Hebrews 11:6

But without _____ it is impossible to please him: for he that cometh to God must _____ that he is, and that he is a _____ of them that diligently _____ him.

> believe   rewarder   faith   seek

65. Hebrews 12:1–2

Wherefore seeing we also are compassed about with so great a cloud of _____, let us lay aside every weight, and the sin which doth so easily beset us, and let us run with patience the race that is set before us, Looking unto Jesus the author and _____ of our faith; who for the joy that was set before him endured the _____, despising the _____, and is set down at the right hand of the throne of God.

> finisher   shame   witnesses   cross

66. Hebrews 13:5

   Let your _____ be without _____; and be _____ with such things as ye have: for he hath said, I will never leave thee, nor forsake thee.

   covetousness   conversation   content

67. James 1:2–3

   My _____, count it all joy when ye fall into divers _____; Knowing this, that the trying of your _____ worketh patience.

   temptations   faith   brethren

68. James 1:12

   _____ is the man that endureth temptation: for when he is tried, he shall receive the crown of _____, which the Lord hath _____ to them that _____ him.

   life   blessed   promised   love

69. James 5:16

   Confess your faults one to another, and pray one for another, that ye may be _____. The effectual fervent _____ of a righteous _____ _____ much.

   prayer   healed   availeth   man

70. 1 Peter 2:24

   Who his own self bare our sins in his own body on the _____, that we, being dead to _____, should live unto _____: by whose _____ ye were healed.

   righteousness   tree   stripes   sins

71. 1 Peter 3:15–16

But sanctify the Lord God in your _____: and be ready always to give an answer to every man that asketh you a reason of the hope that is in you with meekness and fear: Having a good _____; that, whereas they speak evil of you, as of _____, they may be ashamed that falsely accuse your good conversation in _____.

Christ   hearts   evildoers   conscience

72. 1 Peter 5:7

_____ all your _____ upon him; for he careth for _____.

you   casting   care

73. 1 John 1:9

If we confess our _____, he is _____ and just to forgive us our sins, and to cleanse us from all _____.

faithful   unrighteousness   sins

74. 1 John 3:16

Hereby perceive we the love of _____, because he laid down his _____ for us: and we ought to lay down our lives for the _____.

brethren   God   life

75. Revelation 1:10

I was in the _____ on the Lord's _____, and heard behind me a great _____, as of a _____.

trumpet   Spirit   voice   day

WORD SEARCHES

Word searches are fun. In these puzzles, words are placed horizontally, vertically, and diagonally, both forward and backward. Some words may overlap in the puzzle. Simply circle the words in the list in whatever direction they appear. But here's the Bible brilliant twist. For the first two word searches of a topic, you will have the list of words. For the third puzzle of the series, you will not have the list of words but must still find them all.

38

Names of God Part 1

Find the Bible words for God in this puzzle. If you find all the words, give yourself 10 points on the score card.

```
Q U E M U N M G R E A T I A M
H H S G N I K F O G N I K Y K
G A W R C B H Y U C L A V G D
V I N N E T S G X U R H Y A Z
H S H W P T D O G F O B M A L
Y S R O I V A S H L A L P H A
A E F V A N F W Y L K J S T Z
S M T E S C S S G K C Y Q S P
H Y V H A E P A C N E M B I G
E Q K Y E I J O U O I I F R R
W V Q M R V R Y E M V V V H E
A Q Z I G E I K V E D Y I C H
T B T H H N Q N P G J G D L G
A B M T G D S F E A T A T O D
G O O D S H E P H E R D D T R
```

ALPHA	KING OF KINGS	SAVIOR
CHRIST	LAMB OF GOD	THE ROCK
GOOD SHEPHERD	LIVING WATER	THE VINE
GREAT I AM	MESSIAH	YASHEWA
HOLY SPIRIT	OMEGA	

39

Names of God Part 2

Here are the same names of God but in a different puzzle. If you find all the words, give yourself 10 points on the score card.

```
P M R O I V A S F K N H J D L
U H E F B R H T R K J R F N F
S F D S T I R I P S Y L O H D
U G O I S Q O O F K I F A Y R
O B N J Z I J W H C I J Y A E
L W V I Y L A J L O P V N S T
A K K H K K L H C R H P O H A
M K Z V P F T A M E L J E E W
B Q G V L S O A M H N V L W G
O U G X I F I G O T I T E A N
F R Y R O T T S N N S Y U W I
G T H M A S H N E I B Z E C V
O C E E J I F I U A K U H X I
D G R A H P L A F V W W H D L
A G O O D S H E P H E R D F A
```

ALPHA   KING OF KINGS   SAVIOR
CHRIST   LAMB OF GOD   THE ROCK
GOOD SHEPHERD   LIVING WATER   THE VINE
GREAT I AM   MESSIAH   YASHEWA
HOLY SPIRIT   OMEGA

Names of God Part 3

Try to find the same fourteen names for God as you did in the previous two word searches, but this time you do not have the words. If you are successful, give yourself 25 points.

```
L  I  V  I  N  G  W  A  T  E  R  O  N  N  J
G  O  O  D  S  H  E  P  H  E  R  D  K  D  Z
A  Z  I  X  V  P  I  V  N  E  R  A  L  T  Z
H  G  J  E  F  J  K  W  F  U  H  U  I  W  E
P  F  Q  N  S  A  V  I  O  R  K  R  U  C  H
L  J  S  I  J  M  A  M  Y  K  I  T  H  M  S
A  W  D  V  P  B  E  I  B  P  N  A  Z  A  S
M  Z  E  E  D  G  N  D  S  V  G  G  M  G  G
B  A  D  H  A  K  W  Y  K  C  O  R  E  H  T
O  D  W  T  U  B  L  E  I  C  F  E  S  R  P
F  W  G  E  L  O  M  F  H  X  K  A  S  B  Z
G  Q  O  B  H  I  L  R  U  X  I  T  I  W  W
O  H  X  J  X  S  I  W  T  V  N  I  A  H  A
D  K  I  F  X  S  A  G  U  K  G  A  H  W  H
D  G  Y  K  T  D  B  Y  J  E  S  M  K  P  Y
```

People and Angels Part 1

Find the following names of people and angels. If you find all the words, give yourself 10 points.

```
C O R N E L I U S O X Q A T G
I Z A C H A R I A S J E M P U
D S R A B G S E M A N O A H Y
G A A N V F E N Q M W C P L E
S I N I R J R K Q U T H F Q L
G U D I A Z A F Q C X A A J I
L Z K E E H P P L U N P B I J
X O A K O L H E L N H A R V A
M T H J J N I Q A B G Q A R H
I Y A R O R M O B C J D H U E
C I H A B S J C X B A L A A M
H Q A A N A E A B U J I M Y T
A F G H V H S P C U K O A O V
E L A Z A R U S H O Y U H O B
L T R D Z E S P M Y B C I N E
```

ABRAHAM (Genesis 22:11, 15)
BALAAM (Numbers 22:31)
CORNELIUS (Acts 10:3)
DANIEL (Daniel 6:22)
ELIJAH (2 Kings 1:3, 15)
GABRIEL (Luke 1:19, 26)
GIDEON (Judges 6:11, 22)

HAGAR (Genesis 21:17)
ISAIAH (Isaiah 6:2, 6)
JACOB (Genesis 31:11; 32:1)
JESUS (Matthew 4:11)
JOANNA (Luke 24:4–10)
JOHN (Revelation 1:1)
JOSEPH (Matthew 2:13)

LAZARUS (Luke 16:20–22)
MANOAH (Judges 13:13–21)
MICHAEL (Jude 1:9; Revelation 12:7)
SERAPHIM (Isaiah 6:2, 6)
ZACHARIAS (Luke 1:12)

People and Angels Part 2

Once again, find the names of people and angels. Give yourself 10 points if you find them all.

```
D L W V N S G B L A Z A R U S
A M H H U P E Z R I F N V H Q
N E O S W R C R U R B V G X R
I J J Z Y J I S A I A H N H V
E Y S P K I T G E P W G N S E
L E B A L A A M A O H R U V J
H L V D Z H Y L A B M I O U O
K Y D J A T E Z J N L N M R S
G J J V C A G I D E O N A B E
A Q E O H I Y X N F N A B Y P
B R G C A Z Q R B E Y S H Y H
R T I K R N O L A B R A H A M
I M H J I C N J E S U S I K I
E U V Q A U U A D H J A C O B
L S I O S N E L I J A H O T R
```

ABRAHAM	GABRIEL	JESUS	MANOAH
BALAAM	GIDEON	JOANNA	MICHAEL
CORNELIUS	HAGAR	JOHN	SERAPHIM
DANIEL	ISAIAH	JOSEPH	ZACHARIAS
ELIJAH	JACOB	LAZARUS	

People and Angels Part 3

Give yourself 25 points if you find all nineteen hidden names.

```
A K J S R Z A C H A R I A S M
B U T A C T P L P T K S F U I
R W G J C G H D T W B A R N C
A A K G K O B M N J B I E Z H
H J S E E K B M A N O A H T A
A C O Q L A V S V G L H X C E
M U E S D I S O A I I X N O L
U V N I E U J N R D T G Q R U
J R D H R P N A E E G A S N D
H J F A E A H S H O E B B E A
A H Z A O O U K N N J R A L N
H A I J Y S E Q A Q B I L I I
L N W M E W M J Z K L E A U E
V Y H J X L L F E I L L A S L
U K I Z S E R A P H I M M X O
```

The Book of Genesis

A thorough knowledge of the Bible's first book is essential to being truly Bible brilliant. The following questions follow a precise chapter-by-chapter order, hitting the most important parts of each of the fifty chapters. Give yourself 3 points for each correct answer (there are 257 questions in all).

Chapter 1

1. What was created on the first day?
2. What was created on the second day?
3. What was created on the third day?
4. What was created on the fourth day?
5. What was created on the fifth day?
6. What was created on the sixth day?
7. What happened on the seventh day?

Chapter 2

1. From what substance was Adam formed?
2. From what were the animals and birds formed?
3. From which human body part was Eve formed?
4. What place did God give Adam as a home?

Chapter 3

1. Adam and Eve were forbidden to eat from which tree?

2. Who deceived Eve into eating from the tree?

3. How did God curse the serpent for his trickery?

4. What curse did God put on the man?

5. What curse did God put on the woman?

6. Why did God place the cherubims at the east of the Garden of Eden?

7. Why was a flaming sword placed to guard the tree of life?

Chapter 4

1. Why did God reject Cain's offering?

2. What did Cain do to Abel?

3. What did God do to Cain for committing this heinous crime?

4. Why was Cain so worried about God's judgment on him?

5. What did God do to alleviate Cain's worry?

6. Who was born to Adam and Eve after the loss of their son Abel?

Chapter 5

1. Who were Noah's sons?

Chapter 6

1. What did the sons of God do against God's wishes?

2. How did God view the world he created?

3. How did God feel about his creation?

4. What man did God find righteous?

5. What did God instruct the righteous man to do?

6. What were the dimensions of the ark?

7. How many of each animal were to be taken on the ark?

Chapter 7

1. How many of each unclean animal were taken on the ark?

2. How many of each clean animal were taken on the ark?

3. How many of each bird were taken on the ark?

4. How many days did it rain on the earth?

5. How many people were on the ark?

6. Where were the animals of the seas during the voyage of the ark?

Chapter 8

1. After it stopped raining, how many days did the ark float on water?

2. How many months passed before the water receded enough to make mountains visible?

3. In which month of the year did the earth finally become dry again?

Chapter 9

1. What did God consider justice if a man was killed by another man or a beast?

2. What symbol did God provide to show he would never destroy the earth by flood again?

3. What was Ham's reaction to seeing his father drunk and unclothed?

Chapter 10

1. Nimrod was from the line of which of Noah's sons?
2. Where did Japheth's line live?
3. Where did Shem's line live?
4. Whose lines formed the various nations?

Chapter 11

1. What monstrosity did the people decide to build?
2. Why did they want to build the monstrosity?
3. What did God do to foil them?
4. How many years after the flood was Abram born?
5. Who was Lot?

Chapter 12

1. What did God instruct Abram to do?
2. What promise did God make to Abram?
3. What land did God promise Abram?
4. Why did God send plagues on Pharaoh's house?

Chapter 13

1. What problem was caused because of Abram's and Lot's livestock?
2. How was the problem solved?
3. Where did Abram decide to go?
4. Where did Lot decide to go?

Chapter 14

1. When the kings went to war, who was taken captive?
2. Who rescued him?

3. What did Abram do with some of the spoils of war he won in battle?

4. Who witnessed Abram's tithing?

5. What did the king of Sodom offer to Abram?

6. Why did Abram reject the king's offer?

Chapter 15

1. Who was Eliezer?

2. What did God reveal to Abram about his descendants?

3. What horrible thing would happen to Abram's descendants?

4. How long would this horrible thing last?

5. What place would be God's gift to Abram's descendants?

Chapter 16

1. Sarai advised her husband, Abram, to have children with whom?

2. How did Sarai feel toward Hagar after Hagar gave birth?

3. What promise did God make to Hagar?

4. What was the name of Hagar's son?

Chapter 17

1. When Abram was ninety-nine years old, to what did God change his name?

2. What did Abram's new name mean?

3. What was the sign of the covenant between God and Abraham?

4. To what was Sarai's name changed?

5. What did God promise Abraham through Sarah?

Chapter 18

1. While sitting in his tent, what did Abraham see?
2. Whom did Abraham realize his visitors were?
3. What did the visitors tell Abraham about Sarah?
4. What was Sarah's response?
5. What place was considered very evil and was about to be destroyed?
6. What worried Abraham about Lot?

Chapter 19

1. How many of the angels went to Sodom?
2. Who met the angels when they arrived in Sodom?
3. Who gathered outside of Lot's house?
4. What did the people outside of Lot's house want?
5. What did the angels do to the men?
6. Who had sent the men to Sodom?
7. What were they commanded to do to Sodom?
8. What did Lot's sons-in-law think of Lot's dire warning about Sodom's demise?
9. Where did Lot and his family flee to?
10. Who looked back at the burning city of Sodom despite warnings not to?
11. What happened to her?
12. What did Lot's daughters plot to do to him?
13. Why did they make this plot?
14. What two groups are the descendants of Lot?

Chapter 20

1. Why did Abraham call Sarah his sister in Gerar?
2. Who prevented King Abimelech from touching Sarah?
3. After Sarah was returned to Abraham, what happened to Abimelech's household?

Chapter 21

1. What did Abraham and Sarah name their son?
2. What does the name of their son mean?
3. What did Sarah tell Abraham to do with Hagar and her son?
4. What did God tell Hagar he would do for her son?
5. What was the covenant between Abraham and Abimelech?

Chapter 22

1. Why did God command Abraham to sacrifice his son?
2. Who carried the wood for the sacrifice?
3. How did God know that Abraham really did fear him?
4. What did God provide for Abraham to sacrifice instead of his son?
5. In whom would the nations be blessed?
6. Who was Rebekah's father?

Chapter 23

1. Where did Sarah die?
2. Where was Sarah buried?

Chapter 24

1. Whom did Abraham send to find a wife for Isaac?
2. Who met Abraham's servant at the well?
3. How was the servant to distinguish which woman the Lord sent for Isaac?
4. What did Rebekah do when she saw Isaac?
5. Did Isaac approve of Rebekah?

Chapter 25

1. Where was Abraham buried?
2. What did God tell Rebekah about the babies she carried in her womb?
3. What were her children's names?
4. What do the names of her children mean?
5. Who was Isaac's favorite son?
6. Why was Isaac's favorite son his favorite?
7. What did Jacob take from Esau by trickery?

Chapter 26

1. Isaac and Rebekah were in which town?
2. Isaac tried to pass off Rebekah as which of his relatives?
3. Who spotted Isaac and Rebekah while looking through his window?
4. When Isaac became very rich, what did King Abimelech advise him to do?
5. In what town did the Lord bless Isaac?

Chapter 27

1. What was Isaac's blessing for his son Jacob?
2. What was Isaac's blessing for his son Esau?
3. What did Esau swear to do to Jacob after Isaac's death?
4. Where did Rebekah send Jacob?
5. Why did she send Jacob away?

Chapter 28

1. Isaac sent Jacob to marry one of the daughters of whom?
2. What did Jacob dream about on the way to Haran?
3. What was Jacob promised in his dream?
4. What was the name Jacob gave this place?
5. What does the name of the place mean?

Chapter 29

1. How was Rachel related to Jacob?
2. What was Rachel's profession?
3. What did Jacob ask from Laban as payment for his hard labor?
4. Whom did Laban give to Jacob as a wife?
5. How much longer did Jacob serve Laban before he could marry Rachel?
6. What were the names of Leah's first four sons?

Chapter 30

1. Before Rachel conceived, what three people had children for Jacob?
2. What were the names of Leah's next two sons?
3. What was the name of Leah's daughter?

4. What was the name of Rachel's son?
5. Why did Laban want Jacob to stay in the land and not leave?
6. After marriage, what did Jacob want as wages?
7. What did Jacob use to help his livestock multiply?

Chapter 31

1. Who told Jacob to leave Laban's household?
2. What did Rachel take from Laban's house?
3. Where did Rachel hide the stolen goods?
4. How many years in all had Jacob stayed with Laban?

Chapter 32

1. Why did Jacob divide his possessions and people into two groups?
2. Why did Jacob send gifts to Esau?
3. With whom did Jacob think he had wrestled?
4. What happened to the sinew in Jacob's hip as a result of the wrestling?

Chapter 33

1. When Esau saw Jacob, what was his reaction to Jacob?
2. Why didn't Jacob travel to Seir at the same pace as Esau?
3. Where did Jacob finally pitch his tent?
4. From whom did Jacob buy land?

Chapter 34

1. What did Shechem do to Dinah, Jacob's daughter?
2. How did Jacob's sons react upon learning of what had happened to Dinah?

3. Who was Shechem's father?

4. What did Shechem's father suggest they do to remedy the situation?

5. What did Jacob's sons demand be done to all the men in the city?

6. What did Jacob's sons do to the men of the city of Shechem?

Chapter 35

1. Where did God instruct Jacob to go?

2. To what did God change Jacob's name?

3. What does the name Israel mean?

4. Rachel died while doing what?

5. Who was the last child born of Rachel?

6. With whom did Reuben lie, which was immoral?

7. How old was Isaac when he died?

8. What two people buried Isaac?

Chapter 36

1. From what land did Esau choose his wives?

2. What other name did Esau have?

3. From what son of Isaac did the Amalekites originate?

Chapter 37

1. Why did Jacob love Joseph more than his other children?

2. What special garment did Jacob make for Joseph?

3. Why did Joseph's brothers despise him?

4. What did the brothers do in Joseph's dream that was demeaning to them?

5. What did Joseph's brothers plot to do to him?

6. What brother did not want to take part in the plot against Joseph?

7. What did the brothers do to Joseph?

8. Where did the Ishmaelites take Joseph?

9. What did the brothers tell their father, Jacob, about Joseph?

Chapter 38

1. Who killed Judah's sons Er and Onan?

2. Whom did Judah promise to Tamar as a husband?

3. How many children did Tamar have?

Chapter 39

1. Where was Joseph taken as a slave?

2. Who became Joseph's master?

3. What position did Joseph hold in his master's house?

4. What did the master's wife want from Joseph?

5. How did Joseph respond to the advances?

6. What false accusation did the master's wife bring against Joseph?

7. Where was Joseph sent because of the accusation?

8. What position did Joseph have while in prison?

Chapter 40

1. What two people were thrown into prison with Joseph?

2. What was the meaning of the chief butler's dream?

3. What was the meaning of the chief baker's dream?

4. What did Joseph ask of the chief butler?

Chapter 41

1. When Pharaoh had his dream, how many years had passed since the chief butler had gotten out of prison?
2. What did Joseph say Pharaoh's dream meant?
3. What did Joseph recommend Pharaoh do as a result of the dream?
4. Who was the only person ranked higher than Joseph in the land?
5. How old was Joseph when he was placed over Egypt?

Chapter 42

1. Who was left behind when Joseph's ten brothers went to Egypt?
2. Why did they leave the brother behind?
3. What was Joseph's official title in the land of Egypt?
4. What did Joseph accuse his brothers of being?
5. What did Joseph do to his brothers?
6. How long were Joseph's brothers in prison?
7. Why did Joseph's brothers think that prison was retribution against them?
8. When the brothers were released and went back home, who did Joseph keep back?

Chapter 43

1. When did Jacob decide to let his sons go back to Egypt?
2. What did he give his sons to take to Egypt?
3. Why were the brothers frightened of Joseph's dinner invitation?
4. What did Joseph do when he saw Benjamin?

5. What was the seating order for Joseph's brothers?
6. How did Joseph treat Benjamin?

Chapter 44

1. What did Joseph command his steward to put in Benjamin's sack?
2. What did Joseph request Benjamin become to him?
3. What did Joseph's brothers do when they became aware of Joseph's wishes for Benjamin?
4. What did Judah tell Joseph his father would do if he found out about Joseph's request for Benjamin?

Chapter 45

1. When Joseph revealed to his brothers who he was, how did they react?
2. Whom did Joseph tell his brothers had elevated him to such a status?
3. Who approved of Joseph's family moving to Egypt?

Chapter 46

1. After his sons returned from Egypt, who spoke to Jacob in a dream?
2. Who was Joseph's Egyptian wife?
3. Where was Jacob told to go in the dream?
4. To what land did Jacob and his family go?

Chapter 47

1. When their money was exhausted, how did the people pay Joseph for grain?
2. What was the next method of payment for people to buy grain?

3. How long did Jacob get to be with Joseph before Jacob died?

4. What did Jacob ask Joseph to promise him upon his death?

Chapter 48

1. What were the names of Joseph's two sons?

2. Which of Joseph's sons did Jacob bless first?

3. What was Jacob's blessing for Joseph?

Chapter 49

1. What was Reuben's harsh blessing?

2. Why did Reuben receive such a harsh blessing?

3. What did Jacob say would happen to Simeon and Levi?

4. What was Judah's blessing?

5. From which son would the stone of Israel come?

6. Where did Jacob wish to be buried?

7. What other five notable people were buried in the same place?

Chapter 50

1. What did Joseph's brothers fear after their father died?

2. Why did Joseph sob when the messengers came from the brothers?

3. What did Joseph ask his people to do on his behalf when he died?

SECTION 3

THE BIBLE BRILLIANT SECTION

This final large section is the Bible scholar section. It has the most difficult challenges but offers the greatest rewards. Expect nothing easy here, but your sense of satisfaction at answering these questions will be the highest of at any point during your Bible brilliant experience. (Answers to section 3 begin on page 258.)

> I wish to see the Bible study as much a matter of course in the secular colleges as in the seminary. No educated man can afford to be ignorant of the Bible, and no uneducated man can afford to be ignorant of the Bible.
>
> Theodore Roosevelt, twenty-sixth president of the United States

There is nothing in this world that can compare with the Christian fellowship; nothing that can satisfy but Christ.

John D. Rockefeller, American business
magnate and philanthropist

The New Testament is the greatest Book the world has ever known or ever will know.

Charles Dickens, renowned author

FOUR GROUPS OF TRIVIA

Each of the following groups of trivia contains fifty questions. Do one group at a time and give yourself 5 points for each correct answer. You may do any or all of the groups as many times as necessary to achieve your goal. Record your score for each group on the score card.

Group 1

1. How long was Solomon the king over Israel?
2. In the Sermon on the Mount, what did Jesus say would happen to the meek?
3. Into what did Jesus say the merchants had turned his house of prayer?
4. What relation was Annas to Caiaphas?
5. What was the first plague God inflicted on Egypt?
6. "He leadeth me beside the still waters" is a part of what psalm?
7. Who, full of good works and acts of charity, was raised from the dead by Peter?
8. According to James, what is pure and undefiled religion?
9. How many churches were there in Asia Minor in Revelation?
10. In the new Jerusalem, where are the names of the twelve tribes written?
11. In the parable of the ten virgins, what were they waiting for?
12. What did Daniel do for Nebuchadnezzar that no one else could do?
13. When people brought their young children to Jesus, what did the disciples do?

14. Where did Moses meet his future wife for the very first time?

15. Who wrote the majority of the book of Psalms?

16. Of the ten lepers Jesus healed, what nationality was the one who returned to give thanks?

17. What occurred to facilitate the release of Paul and Silas from prison?

18. What did Gideon place on the floor in order to receive a sign from God?

19. In Revelation, what was on the head of the woman clothed with the sun?

20. At what time during their prison stay did Paul and Silas pray and sing to God?

21. What prophet anointed David as king?

22. Who did Jesus say are the two most important people to love?

23. Who was compared to the lilies of the field?

24. What was Jesus's final command to his disciples?

25. What does a soft answer turn away?

26. How did Bathsheba's husband Uriah die?

27. At the temple gate called Beautiful, Peter and John healed a man of what?

28. What did Daniel and his three companions eat and drink instead of the king's meat and drink?

29. What happened to Jesus the eighth day after his birth?

30. What prisoner did the crowd want to be released instead of Jesus?

31. What tribe of Israel looked after the religious aspects of life?

32. Why did Moses's hand become leprous?

33. When Jacob and Esau were in the womb, what did God say they were?

34. What did God do on the seventh day?

35. According to James, how should we treat the rich and the poor?

36. In which city in Judah did Cyrus tell the Israelites to build the temple?

37. What did Jesus say is the first commandment in the law?

38. What did Saul see on his way to Damascus?

39. What job did the prodigal son resort to after spending his inheritance?

40. When Paul was shipwrecked on Malta, how many people from the ship drowned?

41. Where was Paul when he wrote the letter to Philemon?

42. Which region was specially noted for its balm?

43. Who watched over the coats of the men who stoned Stephen?

44. When a man asked Jesus, "Who is my neighbor?" with what parable did Jesus reply?

45. When speaking to the woman at the well, how did Jesus say true worshipers should worship God?

46. How long did Jonah say it would be before Nineveh would be overthrown?

47. How many plagues did God send on Egypt?

48. What was the profession of Zebedee, the father of James and John?

49. What missionary was said to have known the Holy Scriptures from an early age?

50. Who admonished, "Repent ye: for the kingdom of heaven is at hand"?

Group 2

1. What is the root of all evil?
2. Who was Joseph's master in Egypt?
3. The Ethiopian eunuch was reading from which book of prophecy?
4. Who laid hands on Saul of Tarsus and cured him of the blindness he received on the road to Damascus?
5. Whom did Jesus raise from the dead with a prayer of thanks to God?
6. After Aaron turned his rod into a serpent before Pharaoh, what happened to the serpents conjured up by Pharoah's magicians?
7. What did Elisha do for the Shunammite's son?
8. What did Joseph want to do when he discovered Mary was pregnant?
9. What does the law say to do when you see a bird in its nest?
10. Where was Paul from?
11. Where was Jesus crucified?
12. Who said, "When I was a child, I spake as a child"?
13. Whom was Paul with when he wrote the letter to Philemon?
14. The king's wrath is as the roaring of what?
15. When Herod killed all the babies in Bethlehem, to which country did Mary and Joseph escape?

16. What did Boaz claim that Naomi was selling?

17. What did Joseph send to his father from Egypt?

18. How does Psalm 1 start?

19. What object was featured in Jacob's dream at Bethel?

20. What book of the Bible comes before Philemon?

21. What judge was betrayed to the Philistines by a woman?

22. What tribe of Israel did not receive an inheritance of land?

23. Who spotted the baby Moses in the Nile River?

24. What was the name of Ruth's son?

25. In addition to gold and silver, what was Abram rich in?

26. In Nebuchadnezzar's dream, what destroyed the statue of different metals?

27. Martha and Mary lived in what town?

28. Who were Joseph's parents?

29. What happened to forty-two children who made fun of Elisha's baldness?

30. With what ailment was Peter's mother-in-law sick?

31. What were the names of Elimelech's two sons?

32. Who was Bathsheba's first husband?

33. What happens if you break one commandment of the law, according to James?

34. How much of Elijah's spirit did Elisha receive?

35. The baby Jesus remained in Egypt with his parents until what event happened?

36. What animal did Samson kill on his way to Timnah?

37. What came out of a fire and attacked Paul on Malta?

38. What king took possession of Naboth's vineyard?

39. What land did the Lord promise to Abram?

40. Who told her daughter to ask for the head of John the Baptist?

41. Who stole her father's household gods?

42. Why were Shadrach, Meshach, and Abednego thrown into the fiery furnace?

43. For how many days did Jesus appear to his disciples after his resurrection?

44. In the parable of the sower, what was the seed?

45. Out of the ten lepers healed by Jesus, how many came back to thank him?

46. What happened to the man who had no wedding robe in the parable of the marriage feast?

47. What was the name of Ruth's second husband?

48. What unusual trait was common among the seven hundred soldiers who could sling a stone and hit their target every time?

49. Who said that a census of the entire Roman world should be taken at the time of Jesus's birth?

50. How did the wise men know that Jesus had been born?

47

Group 3

1. The fear of the Lord is the beginning of knowledge, but what do fools despise?
2. What was the source of Samson's strength?
3. What sea did the Israelites cross to escape from the Egyptians?
4. What is more difficult than a camel going through the eye of a needle?
5. How many years did the Israelites wander in the wilderness?
6. What does a good tree bring forth?
7. What small body part has the ability to boast of great things?
8. How were sins forgiven in the Old Testament?
9. How does James say we should wait for the coming of the Lord?
10. How is man tempted?
11. Bethlehem is referred to as "little" among the thousands of what place?
12. John was on what island when he was given the vision of Revelation?
13. What type of animal spoke to Balaam?
14. Naaman was told to wash in what river to rid himself of leprosy?

15. To whom did Pilate send Jesus after he finished interrogating him?

16. Why did Jacob and his family seek a new life in Egypt?

17. The blessed man will be like a tree planted by what?

18. Daniel had a dream about what four great things?

19. How were the Thessalonians told to pray?

20. What bizarre things happened to King Nebuchadnezzar before he was restored as king?

21. What is the last book of the Old Testament?

22. What miracle had Jesus just performed when he said, "It is I; be not afraid"?

23. What horrific disaster occurred when Abram and Sarai arrived in the land of Canaan?

24. What was Peter doing when he denied Jesus for the second of three times?

25. Why were the Pharisees upset when Jesus forgave the sins of the sick man lowered through a roof?

26. How was Isaac's wife chosen for him?

27. How old was Abraham when his son Isaac was born?

28. In the parable of the sower, what did the seed that fell among thorns represent?

29. What did Jonah do while he waited to see what would happen to Nineveh?

30. What happened to Daniel after he loudly gave thanks to God by his open window?

31. After the priests blew their trumpets, what happened to the city of Jericho?

32. What was the name of Abraham's nephew?

33. Where did Jonah attempt to flee to instead of going to Nineveh as God had commanded?

34. What disciple did Paul commend for having the same faith his mother, Eunice, had?

35. Why did Solomon turn away from God when he became old?

36. Whose father was so delighted to see him that he gave him his best robe and killed a fatted calf?

37. What did the Pharisee thank God for in the parable of the Pharisee and the publican?

38. After Israel split into two kingdoms after the reign of King Solomon, what kingdom was in the south?

39. What did the shepherds do after they visited the baby Jesus?

40. What chorus in Psalm 136 is repeated in every verse?

41. How did Jonah react to the way the people of Nineveh responded to God's message?

42. To what garden did Jesus go to pray before his arrest?

43. Who carried the cross part of the way for Christ?

44. What woman did Paul send to Rome, requesting that she be given a welcome worthy of the saints?

45. Who was Jonah's father?

46. Which son of Solomon succeeded him as king?

47. How many times did Jesus say you should forgive your brother when he sins against you?

48. In what city did Jesus spend his childhood?

49. On what mountains did Noah's ark finally come to rest?

50. What did the mother of James and John ask of Jesus?

Group 4

1. What was Lot in relation to Abram?
2. Who was instructed by God to leave his home and family to travel to a strange land?
3. Who traveled back to Jerusalem after the captivity to urge the people to rebuild the walls of the city?
4. Whose mother made him a coat year after year?
5. What did an angel tell Zacharias and Elisabeth their son would be called?
6. In what manner did the people listening to the Sermon on the Mount think that Jesus taught?
7. How did Jesus say we should receive the kingdom of God?
8. What did the dove bring back to Noah on the ark?
9. What question concerning marriage did the Pharisees use to try to trap Jesus?
10. What was Jesus teaching about when he said, "What therefore God hath joined together, let not man put asunder"?
11. What female judge described herself as a mother in Israel?
12. What judge killed Eglon, the king of Moab?
13. What two tribes of Israel were not named after sons of Jacob?
14. Who was the first apostle to perform a miracle in the name of Jesus?

15. What person will the "least person in the kingdom of God" be greater than?

16. What does faith require to make it a living faith?

17. How did Korah and his family die?

18. How does Paul tell us to work out our own salvation?

19. How many books are there in the New Testament?

20. In a parable told by Jesus, what did the rich man do after he had a plentiful harvest?

21. In the Lord's Prayer, what follows "hallowed be thy name"?

22. Gabriel, an angel of the Lord, appeared to Mary during what month of Elisabeth's pregnancy?

23. What valuable things did the queen of Sheba give to Solomon?

24. What happened to anyone whose name was not written in the book of life?

25. What did Jesus advise to do if someone asks you to go with them for a mile?

26. According to Peter, what covers a multitude of sins?

27. What did Jesus say about tomorrow in his Sermon on the Mount?

28. In Jesus's parable, why does a man not put new wine into old bottles?

29. In the parable of the leaven, what was the leaven?

30. What was Philemon to do if his slave owed him anything?

31. What was Jonah doing on a ship while a storm was raging?

32. Who was Isaac's wife?

33. Who replaced Judas Iscariot as a disciple?

34. In the parable of the grain of mustard seed, what did birds do when it became a tree?

35. What does "hope deferred" make sick?

36. Five of the ten virgins did not take enough of what?

37. In what direction was the location of the Garden of Eden?

38. How many books are there in the Old Testament?

39. For whom did Joseph interpret dreams while he was in prison?

40. King Herod was living in what city at the time of Jesus's birth?

41. What birds could the poor use for sacrifices if they could not afford lambs?

42. What did Abraham's son carry for his own sacrifice?

43. What did Joseph command to be placed in Benjamin's sack?

44. Aceldama, the field that Judas Iscariot purchased with his betrayal money, was also known as what?

45. What was the name of Abraham's first wife?

46. According to Old Testament law, in what shouldn't a young goat be cooked?

47. In John's vision of Jesus in Revelation, what came out of Jesus's mouth?

48. In what Bible book do we find Haman, the son of Hammedatha?

49. To what condiment did Jesus compare his disciples?

50. What did Paul do to the soothsayer that angered her masters?

Imprisoned

In this twelve-question quiz, give yourself 5 points for each correct answer.

1. Who experienced a great, rumbling earthquake while in prison?
   A. The butler and the baker
   B. Paul and Silas
   C. Peter
   D. John the Baptist

2. What apostle was imprisoned in Jerusalem for preaching the gospel?
   A. Paul and Barnabas
   B. Matthew and Luke
   C. Peter
   D. Paul and James

3. What relative of Jesus was jailed for daring to criticize King Herod's marriage to Herodias?
   A. Joseph
   B. James
   C. David
   D. John the Baptist

4. Who was sent to prison after being falsely accused of trying to seduce Potiphar's wife?
   A. Joseph
   B. David
   C. Joshua
   D. Absalom

5. Whose brothers were imprisoned after being falsely accused of being spies in Egypt?
   A. Jacob's
   B. David's
   C. Samson's
   D. Joseph's

6. Who was jailed for prophesying that the kingdom of Judah would be destroyed?

A. Nathan

B. Jeremiah

C. Elisha

D. Hanani

7. What king of Judah was put in jail and blinded for resisting Babylonian authority?

A. Rehoboam

B. Manasseh

C. Zedekiah

D. Amaziah

8. Who was jailed for prophesying King Asa's demise?

A. Jeremiah

B. Hanani

C. Isaiah

D. Elijah

9. Who was imprisoned and declared an enemy of the Philistines?

A. Samson

B. Simeon

C. Daniel

D. Barabbas

10. What king of Judah was exiled and jailed in Babylon?

A. Joash

B. Jehoiachin

C. Uzziah

D. Hezekiah

11. Who was imprisoned after he prophesied that King Ahab would face a bitter defeat?

A. Micah

B. Obadiah

C. Jeremiah

D. Micaiah

12. What king of Israel was jailed for refusing to recognize Assyrian authority?

A. Jehu

B. Jehoash

C. Hoshea

D. Shallum

Did You Know?

(SET 5)

Here is the final set of astounding Bible facts.

- The longest word in the Bible is also the longest name. Isaiah 8:1 states, "Moreover the LORD said unto me, Take thee a great roll, and write in it with a man's pen concerning Mahershalalhashbaz."

- King Ahasuerus once had a single feast that lasted for 180 days (Esther 1:3–4).

- The only woman the Bible *commands* us to remember is Lot's wife (Luke 17:32).

- Paul was guarded by 470 soldiers when he was taken to see Governor Felix (Acts 23:23).

- The writings of 2 Kings 19 and Isaiah 37 are so similar that they are almost identical.

- The only time the Bible mentions snow is in reference to Benaiah being killed by a lion on a snowy day (2 Samuel 23:20; 1 Chronicles 11:22).

- Hebrews 11 is known as the "faith hall of fame," as it contains within its pages the following biblical heroes: Abel, Enoch, Noah, Abraham, Sarah, Isaac, Jacob, Joseph, Moses, and Joshua.

TRIVIA BY TOPIC

In the following section, complete each multiple-choice quiz and give yourself 2 points for each correct answer.

51

Fasting

1. After being baptized, who fasted for forty days?
   A. John the Baptist
   B. Peter
   C. John
   D. Jesus

2. Who fasted for forty days while on Mount Sinai?
   A. Jeremiah
   B. Jacob
   C. Moses
   D. Joshua

3. Who was saved from starvation by birds that brought him food?
   A. Elisha
   B. Elijah
   C. Jonah
   D. Joel

4. Who tried to save the life of his and Bathsheba's son by fasting?
   A. Saul
   B. David
   C. Uriah
   D. Esau

5. How many men took an oath to fast until Paul was assassinated?
   A. 3
   B. 12
   C. More than 40
   D. 100

6. Who fasted for 14 days on a ship with 276 passengers?
   A. Paul
   B. Stephen
   C. Peter
   D. John

7. What king fasted after Daniel was thrown into the lions' den?
   A. Darius
   B. Zedekiah
   C. Amon
   D. Uzziah

8. What two apostles prayed and fasted when selecting elders for churches?
   A. Peter and John
   B. Paul and Barnabas
   C. Timothy and Titus
   D. Mark and Luke

9. What Persian court official fasted before approaching the king with a case?
   A. Nehemiah
   B. Obadiah
   C. Jeremiah
   D. Elijah

10. When the people of Jerusalem gathered for a fast, who read the prophecy of Jeremiah?
    A. Baruch
    B. Deborah
    C. Samson
    D. Josiah

52

Wine

1. Whom does the Bible call gluttonous and a winebibber?
   A. Peter
   B. Paul
   C. John the Baptist
   D. Jesus

2. Paul recommended wine for what part of the body?
   A. Head
   B. Leg
   C. Stomach
   D. Back

3. What church official must be "not given to wine," according to Paul?
   A. A bishop
   B. A deacon
   C. A widow
   D. A layman

4. What kind of person should be given wine, according to Proverbs?
   A. A sad or afflicted person
   B. A sick person
   C. A healthy person
   D. A happy person

5. Whose army murdered Zeeb the Midianite at his winepress?
   A. Joshua's
   B. Gideon's
   C. David's
   D. Saul's

6. To whom did the
   Lord say that if a man
   or woman wanted to
   make a special vow of
   dedication to the Lord
   as a Nazirite, they must
   abstain from wine?
   A. Moses
   B. Aaron
   C. Noah
   D. Abraham

7. What was mixed with
   the wine Jesus was
   offered on the cross?
   A. Myrrh
   B. Vinegar or gall
   C. Water
   D. Nutmeg

8. According to Jesus,
   people prefer what type
   of wine?
   A. Fresh wine
   B. Chilled wine
   C. Old wine
   D. Pressed wine

53

The Apostles

1. Who was the first apostle to be martyred?
   A. James
   B. John
   C. Matthew
   D. Peter

2. Who succeeded Judas Iscariot as an apostle?
   A. Jude
   B. Timothy
   C. Matthias
   D. Joseph

3. What apostle was a tax collector from Capernaum?
   A. Matthew
   B. Matthias
   C. Mattathah
   D. Matthan

4. Who was called the beloved disciple?
   A. Matthew
   B. Mark
   C. Luke
   D. John

54

Kings

1. In Israel, what king called Elijah a troublemaker?
   A. Abimelech
   B. Joash
   C. Zebah
   D. Ahab

2. What king had nine hundred iron chariots?
   A. Og
   B. Jabin
   C. Joash
   D. Agag

3. Who was the last king to reign in Israel?
   A. Saul
   B. David
   C. Hoshea
   D. Abijah

4. What king permitted his daughter to marry Ahab?
   A. Ethbaal
   B. Arad
   C. Zedikiah
   D. Agag

5. What king was later destroyed after attacking the Israelites as they made their way to Canaan?
   A. The king of Arad
   B. Agag
   C. King David
   D. King Solomon

6. What ruler of Hazor formed an alliance against Joshua?
   A. Og
   B. Jabin
   C. Joash
   D. Agag

7. What king infamously owned an enormous iron bed?

   A. Ethbaal

   B. Arad

   C. Agag

   D. Og

8. Although he anointed the first two kings, who rebelled against having a king over himself?

   A. Elijah

   B. Elisha

   C. Samuel

   D. Daniel

9. What meager shepherd boy did Samuel make king in front of the boy's brothers?

   A. Joseph

   B. David

   C. Josiah

   D. Joash

10. Nathan was angered by the adulterous activities of what king?

   A. Saul

   B. David

   C. Josiah

   D. Joash

55

Heaven Awaits

1. Who is preparing heaven for all the saints?
   A. Jesus Christ
   B. Angels
   C. The prophets of old
   D. Everyone

2. Who is heaven designed for?
   A. Angels
   B. The devil
   C. Born-again believers
   D. Everyone

3. What describes heaven?
   A. Sunny and bright
   B. The same as earth
   C. A glorious city
   D. None of the above

4. What is the name of the city of God?
   A. The new Jerusalem
   B. The golden city
   C. The city of gold
   D. New Hope City

5. How many foundation stones does the city of God rest upon?
   A. 5
   B. 7
   C. 10
   D. 12

6. What is the wall that surrounds the city made of?
   A. Pure silver
   B. Pure jasper
   C. Pure gold
   D. Pure joy

7. What are gates around the city made of?
   A. Solid brass
   B. Solid jasper
   C. Solid pearl
   D. Solid gold

8. How many varieties of fruit does the tree of life bear?

    A. 12
    B. 2
    C. 7
    D. 5

9. How many thrones (seats) surround the throne of God?

    A. 3
    B. 5
    C. 7
    D. 24

10. How many creatures who worship God continually are beside the throne of God?

    A. 3
    B. 4
    C. 5
    D. 7

11. Of what is the main street of the city of God composed?

    A. Clear glass
    B. Silver
    C. Pearls
    D. Pure gold

12. In heaven, there will be no more what?

    A. Night
    B. Sin
    C. Sickness, pain, or death
    D. All of the above

56

Hairy and Hairless

1. What type of people were forbidden to shave their heads or grow their hair long?
   A. Pharisees
   B. Prophets
   C. Priests
   D. Scribes

2. What Israelite judge never shaved or cut his hair until his mistress did it for him?
   A. Othniel
   B. Barak
   C. Samson
   D. Joseph

3. Who was purified by cutting his hair?
   A. Joseph
   B. Paul
   C. Jonathan
   D. James

4. What king of Babylon once lived in the wilderness and let his hair grow wild?
   A. Daniel
   B. Nebuchadnezzar
   C. Elijah
   D. Naaman

5. Who was the first person in the Bible said to be hairy?
   A. Noah
   B. Abraham
   C. Esau
   D. Joseph

6. Who shaved his head after learning his children had been destroyed?
   A. Noah
   B. Naaman
   C. David
   D. Job

7. Which of David's sons cut his hair once a year, yielding two hundred shekels' worth of hair (nearly six pounds)?
   A. Samson
   B. Solomon
   C. Jonathan
   D. Absalom

8. Who had to shave all his hair twice, six days apart?
   A. An epileptic
   B. A blind person
   C. A leper
   D. A paralytic

9. Who was forbidden to "round the corners of your heads"?
   A. Greeks
   B. Chaldeans
   C. The children of Israel
   D. Egyptians

10. Who is the only man mentioned in the Bible as being naturally bald?
    A. Elijah
    B. Jacob
    C. Elisha
    D. Esau

11. God told what prophet to shave his head and beard?
    A. Isaiah
    B. Jeremiah
    C. Ezekiel
    D. Daniel

12. What prophet was described as a very hairy man?
    A. Elisha
    B. Hosea
    C. Elijah
    D. Amos

WORD FILL

In the following section, divided by topic, simply fill in all the blanks to complete the Scripture passage. Give yourself 5 points for each passage you complete correctly.

57

Encouragement

1. Proverbs 18:10
   The name of the LORD is a strong _____; the righteous
   runneth into it, and is _____.

2. _____ 3:5–6
   _____ in the LORD with all thine _____; and
   lean not unto thine own understanding. In all thy ways
   acknowledge him, and he shall direct thy paths.

3. Isaiah 41:10
   _____ thou not; for I am with thee: be not
   _____; for I am thy God: I will strengthen thee; yea,
   I will help thee; yea, I will uphold thee with the right
   _____ of my righteousness.

4. _____ 14:27
   _____ I leave with you, my peace I give unto you:
   not as the _____ giveth, give I unto you. Let not your
   heart be troubled, neither let it be afraid.

5. _____ 16:33
   These things I have spoken unto you, that in _____
   ye might have peace. In the _____ ye shall have
   tribulation: but be of good cheer; I have overcome the
   world.

6. Psalm 46:1–2

   _____ is our _____ and strength, a very present
   help in trouble. Therefore will not we fear, though the
   earth be removed, and though the _____ be carried
   into the midst of the _____.

7. 2 _____ 1:7

   For God hath not given us the _____ of fear; but of
   _____, and of _____, and of a sound mind.

8. _____ 16:8

   I have set the _____ always before me: because he is
   at my right hand, I shall not be moved.

9. Psalm 55:22

   _____ thy burden upon the _____, and he shall
   sustain thee: he shall never suffer the righteous to be
   moved.

10. 1 _____ 5:7

    Casting all your _____ upon him; for he careth for
    you.

11. Isaiah 26:3

    Thou wilt keep him in _____ peace, whose
    _____ is stayed on thee: because he trusteth in thee.

12. _____ 118:14

    The _____ is my strength and _____, and is
    become my salvation.

13. _____ 119:114

    Thou art my _____ place and my _____: I hope
    in thy word.

14. Psalm 119:25
    My soul cleaveth unto the _____: quicken thou me
    according to thy _____.

15. _____ 119:50
    This is my comfort in my affliction: for thy _____
    hath quickened me.

16. Psalm 119:71
    It is good for me that I have been _____; that I might
    _____ thy statutes.

17. _____ 120:1
    In my _____ I cried unto the _____, and he
    heard me.

58

Friendship

1. Proverbs 18:24
   A man that hath friends must shew himself friendly: and there is a _____ that sticketh closer than a _____.

2. _____ 22:24–25
   Make no friendship with an _____ man; and with a furious man thou shalt not go: Lest thou learn his ways, and get a snare to thy _____.

3. Proverbs 13:20
   He that walketh with _____ men shall be wise: but a companion of _____ shall be destroyed.

4. Proverbs 27:5–6
   Open rebuke is _____ than secret love. Faithful are the wounds of a friend; but the _____ of an enemy are deceitful.

5. Ecclesiastes 4:9–10
   _____ are better than one; because they have a good reward for their labour. For if they fall, the one will lift up his fellow: but woe to him that is alone when he falleth; for he hath not another to _____ him up.

6. _____ 15:12
   This is my commandment, That ye _____ one another, as I have loved you.

7. Proverbs 17:17

   A _____ loveth at all times, and a _____ is born
   for adversity.

8. Proverbs 27:17

   _____ sharpeneth iron; so a _____ sharpeneth
   the countenance of his friend.

9. Proverbs 12:26

   The _____ is more excellent than his neighbour: but
   the way of the _____ seduceth them.

10. James 4:4

   Ye _____ and adulteresses, know ye not that the
   friendship of the _____ is enmity with God?
   whosoever therefore will be a friend of the world is the
   _____ of God.

11. Job 16:20–21

   My _____ scorn me: but mine eye poureth out
   _____ unto God. O that one might plead for a man
   with God, as a man pleadeth for his neighbour!

SECTION 4

THE BONUS SECTION

The nearer I approach to the end of my pilgrimage, the clearer is the evidence of the divine origin of the Bible, and the grandeur and sublimity of God's remedy for fallen man are more appreciated, and the future is illumined with hope and joy.

Francis Bacon, English philosopher, scientist, lawyer, and father of the scientific method

The Book of Revelation

Just as a thorough knowledge of the Bible's first book is essential to becoming Bible brilliant, knowing the final book well is equally essential. Give yourself 10 bonus points for each question you answer correctly as you move through many key points of the book of Revelation chapter by chapter.

Chapter 1

1. Who received this book's revelation from Jesus by way of an angel?
2. Who was called the Alpha and Omega?
3. The book was written to what group of seven?
4. What did the seven stars and seven candlesticks represent?

Chapter 2

1. What was the problem with the church of Ephesus?
2. What was wrong with the church of Smyrna?
3. What church allowed idolatry and immorality?
4. What church was led into uncleanness and immorality by a prophetess?

Chapter 3

1. What church had become a dead church?
2. What church was the faith church that served God well?
3. What type of church was the church of the Laodiceans?

Chapter 4

1. Whom did John see sitting on a throne?
2. What did the seven lamps before the throne represent?
3. What did each of the four living creatures look like?
4. What twenty-four things/people were around the throne?

Chapter 5

1. What was in God's hand?
2. Who was the only one worthy to loose the seals and open the book?

Chapter 6

1. What was the color of the horse of the first seal?
2. What did the red horse of the second seal bring to earth?
3. What did the black horse of the third seal bring to earth?
4. What horse of the fourth seal brought death to a fourth of the earth?
5. Whose souls were revealed because of the fifth seal?
6. What great thing did the sixth seal bring?

Chapter 7

1. What was the number of people sealed?
2. What group was the great multitude before the throne?

Chapter 8

1. What began following the prayers of the saints?
2. What did the first trumpet release?
3. What did the second trumpet bring?
4. The third trumpet initiated the falling of what item from heaven?
5. The fourth trumpet prevented what portion of the sun from giving light?

Chapter 9

1. What did the locusts do to humankind?
2. What did the sixth trumpet release on earth?
3. How large was the army of destruction?
4. Did the rest of humankind repent from their evil?

Chapter 10

1. What did the mighty angel proclaim?
2. After the sounding of the seventh trumpet, what would happen to the mystery of God?

Chapter 11

1. How long was the holy city of Jerusalem to be overrun by the Gentiles?
2. What did the two witnesses do for 1,260 days?
3. Who killed the two witnesses?
4. What happened to the two witnesses after three and a half days?
5. What did the seventh trumpet proclaim?

Chapter 12

1. What did the woman with the twelve stars represent?
2. What was the fiery red dragon?
3. What did John see come down to the earth and sea?
4. Who was the child born to the woman?
5. Who was the woman's other offspring?

Chapter 13

1. The beast John saw was like what animal?
2. What was the beast permitted to do?
3. What rose from out of the earth?
4. What two places did people wear the mark of the beast?

Chapter 14

1. Who stood victorious with Jesus on Mount Zion?
2. What did the first angel proclaim?
3. What angel proclaimed the fall of Babylon?
4. The third angel warned against accepting what?
5. On what did Jesus come?

Chapter 15

1. Who was standing, equipped with harps of God?
2. Seven angels had vials that represented what?

Chapter 16

1. What did the first angel pour out on the earth?
2. What did the second angel cause the sea to turn into?
3. What did the third angel cause the rivers and springs to turn into?
4. What did the fourth angel cause people to be scorched from?
5. What did the fifth angel cause the beast and its kingdom to become full of?
6. What river did the sixth angel cause to dry up?
7. What calamity did the seventh angel cause?

Chapter 17

1. What did the seven heads of the beast represent?
2. What did the ten horns represent?

Chapter 18

1. How long did the judgment of Babylon take?
2. What did one strong angel throw into the sea?

Chapter 19

1. What was completely destroyed as this chapter begins?
2. Who rode the white horse?
3. What was the fate of the beast and the false prophet?

Chapter 20

1. Where was Satan cast and for how long?
2. What first thing did all believers become part of?
3. What was Satan's final fate?
4. Who was judged at the great white throne?

Chapter 21

1. What two new things were created?
2. What came down to earth?
3. Whose names were on the twelve gates of the new Jerusalem?
4. How large was the city?
5. What gem were the walls constructed of in the new Jerusalem?
6. From what were the gates of the new Jerusalem constructed?
7. What lit up the city?

Chapter 22

1. What proceeded from the throne?
2. What sat in the middle of the main street?
3. What does anyone who reads the book of Revelation receive?
4. What is the final word of the Bible?

Crossword Puzzle 2

This crossword puzzle is supersized. Give yourself 50 bonus points if you solve it with five or fewer mistakes.

Across

7. With what Jesus fed 5,000 (3 words)
11. 1 Kings 16:30, And ___ the son of Omri did evil
12. ___ the Bible every day
14. 1 Samuel 14:14, And that first slaughter, which Jonathan and his armourbearer made, was about twenty men, within as it were an half ___ of land
15. Genesis 1:27, So God created man in his own image, in the image of God created he ___
17. Abraham's grandson
19. Jerusalem's region
20. Exodus 16:28, And the Lord said unto Moses, How long refuse ye to keep my commandments and my ___?
21. Jeremiah 2:32, Can a maid forget her ornaments, or a bride her ___?
23. Atone for something, with "oneself"
25. Event in Luke, with "the"
27. Apostle to the Gentiles
28. Psalm 128:3, Thy wife shall be as a fruitful ___ by the sides of thine house

29. Leviticus 19:5, And if ye offer a sacrifice of peace offerings unto the Lord, ye shall offer ___ your own will (2 words)
31. Adam's mate
33. Genesis 17:5, Neither shall thy name ___ more be called Abram
34. What those who believe in Jesus Christ shall have (2 words)
36. Brother of Moses
37. Opposite of loves
39. First paradise (3 words)
41. A female follower of Jesus during his time on earth (2 words)
46. "The evidence of things not seen": Hebrews 11:1
48. Genesis 24:29, And Rebekah ___ brother, and his name was Laban (2 words)
49. Psalm 34:16, The face of the Lord is against them that do ___
50. Greed, envy, or pride
51. Exodus 9:9, And it shall become ___ dust in all the land of Egypt
52. 1 John 2:18, Little children, it is the last time: and as ye have heard that ___ shall come
53. 2 Samuel 22:6, The sorrows of ___ compassed me about; the snares of death prevented me

Down

1. Priest's gown
2. Man ___ wife
3. Standard Holy Bible (3 words)
4. Opposite of he
5. Abraham, Isaac, or Jacob
6. December holiday
8. "Jesus wept" in the Bible
9. Matthew 2:2, For we have seen his ___ in the east
10. 1 Chronicles 16:30, Fear before him, all the earth: the world also shall be ___, that it be not moved
13. Term referring to the Almighty
16. Jesus's early profession
18. Features of some modern Bibles
22. What Jesus calmed (2 words)
24. Beelzebub
26. See 24-Down
30. Father of James and John
31. God, in Hebrew texts
32. Holiday when the hymn "Rise Again" is sung
35. Third book of the New Testament
38. Prophet who anointed Saul and David as kings
39. What was written on the commandments (2 words)
40. Genesis 16:16, And Abram was fourscore and six years old, when Hagar bare ___ to Abram
42. First human
43. 40-day period before Easter
44. Member of the family
45. Three came from the East
46. Go without food purposely
47. Genesis 43:21, And it came to pass, when we came to the ___, that we opened our sacks

Reading the Bible in One Year

Here is a precise schedule for reading the Bible in one year that offers easily digested chunks of God's Word for consistent study. You may start on any date.

Day 1—Genesis 1–3

Day 2—Genesis 4–8

Day 3—Genesis 9–13

Day 4—Genesis 14–17

Day 5—Genesis 18–20

Day 6—Genesis 21–23

Day 7—Genesis 24–26

Day 8—Genesis 27–29

Day 9—Genesis 30–32

Day 10—Genesis 33–35

Day 11—Genesis 36–38

Day 12—Genesis 39–41

Day 13—Genesis 42–44

Day 14—Genesis 45–47

Day 15—Genesis 48–50

Day 16—Exodus 1–3

Day 17—Exodus 4–6

Day 18—Exodus 7–9

Day 19—Exodus 10–12

Day 20—Exodus 13–16

Day 21—Exodus 17–20

Day 22—Exodus 21–23

Day 23—Exodus 24–27

Day 24—Exodus 28–31

Day 25—Exodus 32–34

Day 26—Exodus 35–37

Day 27—Exodus 38–40

Day 28—Leviticus 1–4

Day 29—Leviticus 5–7

Day 30—Leviticus 8–10

Day 31—Leviticus 11–13

Day 32—Leviticus 14–16

Day 33—Leviticus 17–19

Day 34—Leviticus 20–21

Day 35—Leviticus 22–23

Day 36—Leviticus 24–25

Day 37—Leviticus 26–27

Day 38—Numbers 1–2

Day 39—Numbers 3–4

Day 40—Numbers 5–6

Day 41—Numbers 7

Day 42—Numbers 8–10

Day 43—Numbers 11–13

Day 44—Numbers 14–15

Day 45—Numbers 16–18

Day 46—Numbers 19–22

Special References

Alphabetical List of Names of God

Advocate—1 John 2:1

Almighty—Revelation 1:8

Alpha and Omega—Revelation 1:8

Amen—Revelation 3:14

Anointed One—Psalm 2:2

Apostle—Hebrews 3:1

Author and finisher of our faith—Hebrews 12:2

Beginning and end—Revelation 21:6

Beginning of the creation of God—Revelation 3:14

Bishop of your souls—1 Peter 2:25

Branch—Zechariah 3:8

Bread of life—John 6:35, 48

Bridegroom—Matthew 9:15

Carpenter—Mark 6:3

Chief Shepherd—1 Peter 5:4

The Christ—Matthew 1:16

Comforter—Jeremiah 8:18

Consolation of Israel—Luke 2:25

Corner stone—Ephesians 2:20

Dayspring—Luke 1:78

Day star—2 Peter 1:19

Deliverer—Romans 11:26

Desire of all nations—Haggai 2:7

Door of the sheep—John 10:7

Emmanuel—Matthew 1:23

Everlasting Father—Isaiah 9:6

Faithful and true witness—Revelation 3:14

Firstfruits—1 Corinthians 15:23

Foundation—Isaiah 28:16

Fountain—Zechariah 13:1

Friend of publicans and sinners—Matthew 11:19

God—John 1:1

Good shepherd—John 10:11

Governor—Matthew 2:6

Great shepherd—Hebrews 13:20

Guide—Psalm 48:14

Head of the body (church)—Colossians 1:18

High Priest—Hebrews 3:1; 4:15

Holy One of Israel—Isaiah 41:14

Horn of salvation—Luke 1:69

I Am—Exodus 3:14

Jehovah—Psalm 83:18

Jesus—Matthew 1:21

King of Israel—Matthew 27:42

King of Kings—1 Timothy 6:15; Revelation 19:16

Lamb of God—John 1:29

Last Adam—1 Corinthians 15:45

Life—John 11:25

Light of the world—John 8:12; 9:5

Lion of the tribe of Judah—Revelation 5:5

Lord of Lords—1 Timothy 6:15; Revelation 19:16

Master—Matthew 23:8

Mediator—1 Timothy 2:5

Messiah—John 1:41

Mighty God—Isaiah 9:6

Morning star—Revelation 22:16

Nazarene—Matthew 2:23

Our passover—1 Corinthians 5:7

Potentate—1 Timothy 6:15

Prince of Peace—Isaiah 9:6

Prophet—Acts 3:22

Propitiation—1 John 2:2

Purifier—Malachi 3:3

Rabbi—John 1:49

Ransom—1 Timothy 2:6

Redeemer—Isaiah 41:14

Refiner—Malachi 3:3

Refuge—Isaiah 25:4

Resurrection—John 11:25

Righteousness—Jeremiah 23:6

Rock—Deuteronomy 32:4; 2 Samuel 22:47

Root and the offspring of David—Revelation 22:16

Rose of Sharon—Song of Solomon 2:1

Sacrifice—Ephesians 5:2

Saviour—Luke 1:47

Seed of David—2 Timothy 2:8

Seed of the woman—Genesis 3:15

Servant—Isaiah 42:1

Shepherd—1 Peter 2:25

Shiloh—Genesis 49:10

Son of David—Matthew 15:22

Son of God—Luke 1:35

Son of man—Matthew 18:11

Son of Mary—Mark 6:3

Son of the Most High—Luke 1:32

Stone—Isaiah 28:16

Sun of righteousness—Malachi 4:2

Teacher—Matthew 26:18

Truth—John 14:6

Vine—John 15:1

Way—John 14:6

Wonderful Counselor—Isaiah 9:6

Word—John 1:1

The Ten Commandments

1. Thou shalt have no other gods before me. (Exodus 20:3)
2. Thou shalt not make unto thee any graven image, or any likeness of any thing that is in heaven above, or that is in the earth beneath, or that is in the water under the earth. (Exodus 20:4)
3. Thou shalt not take the name of the LORD thy God in vain; for the LORD will not hold him guiltless that taketh his name in vain. (Exodus 20:7)

4. Remember the sabbath day, to keep it holy. (Exodus 20:8)

5. Honour thy father and thy mother: that thy days may be long upon the land which the LORD thy God giveth thee. (Exodus 20:12)

6. Thou shalt not kill. (Exodus 20:13)

7. Thou shalt not commit adultery. (Exodus 20:14)

8. Thou shalt not steal. (Exodus 20:15)

9. Thou shalt not bear false witness against thy neighbour. (Exodus 20:16)

10. Thou shalt not covet thy neighbour's house, thou shalt not covet thy neighbour's wife, nor his manservant, nor his maidservant, nor his ox, nor his ass, nor any thing that is thy neighbour's. (Exodus 20:17)

The Seven "I Am" Statements of Jesus

1. And Jesus said unto them, I am the bread of life. (John 6:35)

2. Then spake Jesus again unto them, saying, I am the light of the world. (John 8:12)

3. Then said Jesus unto them again, Verily, verily, I say unto you, I am the door of the sheep. (John 10:7)

4. I am the good shepherd: the good shepherd giveth his life for the sheep. (John 10:11)

5. Jesus said unto her, I am the resurrection, and the life. (John 11:25)

6. Jesus saith unto him, I am the way, the truth, and the life: no man cometh unto the Father, but by me. (John 14:6)

7. I am the true vine, and my Father is the husbandman. (John 15:1)

The Eight Beatitudes

1. Blessed are the poor in spirit: for theirs is the kingdom of heaven. (Matthew 5:3)
2. Blessed are they that mourn: for they shall be comforted. (Matthew 5:4)
3. Blessed are the meek: for they shall inherit the earth. (Matthew 5:5)
4. Blessed are they which do hunger and thirst after righteousness: for they shall be filled. (Matthew 5:6)
5. Blessed are the merciful: for they shall obtain mercy. (Matthew 5:7)
6. Blessed are the pure in heart: for they shall see God. (Matthew 5:8)
7. Blessed are the peacemakers: for they shall be called the children of God. (Matthew 5:9)
8. Blessed are they which are persecuted for righteousness' sake: for theirs is the kingdom of heaven. (Matthew 5:10)

Scripture Is Inspired by God

1. All Scripture is given by inspiration of God, and is profitable for doctrine, for reproof, for correction, for instruction in righteousness, that the man of God may be perfect, thoroughly furnished unto all good works. (2 Timothy 3:16–17)
2. Knowing this first, that no prophecy of scripture is of any private interpretation. For the prophecy came not in old time by the will of man: but holy men of God spake as they were moved by the Holy Ghost. (2 Peter 1:20–21)

The Twenty-Four Titles of Christ

1. Adam, last Adam (1 Corinthians 15:45)
2. Alpha and Omega (Revelation 21:6)
3. Bread of life (John 6:35)
4. Chief corner stone (Ephesians 2:20)
5. Chief Shepherd (1 Peter 5:4)
6. Emmanuel, God with us (Matthew 1:23)
7. Firstborn from the dead (Colossians 1:18)
8. Good shepherd (John 10:11)
9. Great shepherd of the sheep (Hebrews 13:20)
10. High Priest (Hebrews 3:1)
11. Holy One of God (Mark 1:24)
12. King of Kings, Lord of Lords (Revelation 19:16)
13. Lamb of God (John 1:29)
14. Light of the world (John 9:5)
15. Lion of Judah (Revelation 5:5)
16. Lord of glory (1 Corinthians 2:8)
17. Mediator between God and men (1 Timothy 2:5)
18. Only begotten of the Father (John 1:14)
19. Prophet (Acts 3:22)
20. Saviour (Luke 1:47)
21. Seed of Abraham (Galatians 3:16)
22. Son of God (Mark 1:1)
23. Son of man (Matthew 18:11)
24. The Word (John 1:1)

The Twelve Apostles

1. Simon Peter
2. Andrew (Peter's brother)
3. James (son of Zebedee)
4. John (James's brother)
5. Philip
6. Bartholomew
7. Thomas
8. Matthew
9. James (son of Alphaeus)
10. Thaddaeus
11. Simon
12. Judas Iscariot (After Judas betrayed the Lord Jesus Christ, Matthias was chosen by the other disciples as his replacement.)

Seven Women Who Had Miraculous Births

1. Sarah, Abraham's wife (Genesis 11:30)
2. Rebekah, Isaac's wife (Genesis 25:21)
3. Rachel, Jacob's wife (Genesis 29:31)
4. Samson's mother (Judges 13:2)
5. Hannah, Samuel's mother (1 Samuel 1:5)
6. Elisabeth, the mother of John the Baptist (Luke 1:7)
7. Mary, the virgin mother of Jesus (Luke 1:26–2:20)

Ten People Who Were Raised from the Dead

1. Widow of Zarephath's son, by Elijah (1 Kings 17:22)
2. Shunammite woman's son, by Elisha (2 Kings 4:34–35)

3. The man who came in contact with Elisha's bones (2 Kings 13:20–21)

4. Widow of Nain's son, raised by Jesus (Luke 7:14–15)

5. Jairus's daughter, raised by Jesus (Luke 8:52–56)

6. Lazarus, raised by Jesus (John 11)

7. Jesus (Matthew 28:6; Acts 2:24)

8. The mass of holy people in tombs, when Jesus gave up his spirit (Matthew 27:52–53)

9. Dorcas, by Peter (Acts 9:40)

10. Eutychus, by Paul (Acts 20:9–12)

Witnesses Who Saw Jesus Christ after His Resurrection

1. Mary Magdalene (Mark 16:9)

2. The other women (Matthew 28:9)

3. The two disciples (Luke 24:15)

4. The eleven disciples (Luke 24:36)

5. Peter (1 Corinthians 15:5)

6. Five hundred brethren (1 Corinthians 15:6)

7. Ten disciples (John 20:19)

8. James (1 Corinthians 15:7)

9. Witnesses at his ascension (Luke 24:50)

10. Paul (Acts 9:5; 1 Corinthians 15:8)

Score Card

	Possible Scores	Bonus Points	Your Scores
	3,562	935	
Section 1: The Must-Know Section			
1 Do Not Be Fooled	150		
2 The Essentials	100		
3 Books of the Bible	186		
5 150 Key Verses	300		
All about Money			
6 Maintaining Budgets	20		
7 Debt	18		
8 Wealth	16		
10 Being Happy with What You Have	20		
11 Giving and Being Generous	44		
Specialized Multiple-Choice Trivia			
12 All about Food	12		
13 From Sweet to Bitter	10		
14 Residential Area	12		
15 Kiddie Land	10		
17 Window Display	10		
18 That Makes Scents	10		
19 Nighty-Night	11		
20 Wedding Bells	8		
21 Farming	10		
Scripture Fill in the Blanks			
22 Fill in the Blanks	30		
23 Scriptures on Salvation	12		
24 Scriptures on Security	50		
25 Crossword Puzzle 1		25	

	Possible Scores	Bonus Points	Your Scores
Section 2: The Advanced Section			
Specialized True or False Trivia			
26 Group 1	20		
27 Group 2	20		
28 Group 3	20		
29 Group 4	20		
30 Group 5	20		
31 Group 6	20		
32 Group 7	20		
33 Group 8	20		
34 Group 9	20		
35 Group 10	20		
37 Memory Verses	150		
Word Searches			
38 Names of God Part 1	10		
39 Names of God Part 2	10		
40 Names of God Part 3	25		
41 People and Angels Part 1	10		
42 People and Angels Part 2	10		
43 People and Angels Part 3	25		
44 The Book of Genesis	771		
Section 3: The Bible Brilliant Section			
Four Groups of Trivia			
45 Group 1	250		
46 Group 2	250		
47 Group 3	250		
48 Group 4	250		
49 Imprisoned	60		

	Possible Scores	Bonus Points	Your Scores
Trivia by Topic			
51 Fasting	20		
52 Wine	16		
53 The Apostles	8		
54 Kings	20		
55 Heaven Awaits	24		
56 Hairy and Hairless	24		
Word Fill			
57 Encouragement	85		
58 Friendship	55		
Section 4: The Bonus Section			
59 The Book of Revelation		860	
60 Crossword Puzzle 2		50	

Answers

SECTION 1: THE MUST-KNOW SECTION

---

1. Do Not Be Fooled

1. False, that phrase does not appear in the Bible at all.
2. False, the Bible does not mention an "apple," only "fruit."
3. False, that phrase is from a seventeenth-century poem by Samuel Butler.
4. False, that phrase is from a poem by English poet William Cowper, who was born in 1731.
5. False, that phrase is not written in any book of the Bible.
6. False, the Bible does not give a specific number of wise men.
7. False, "The Little Drummer Boy" is a Christmas carol and is not based on any biblical character.
8. False, according to Jonah 1:17, Jonah was in the belly of "a great fish."
9. False, the Bible never mentions Satan taking the form of or entering into the serpent in the Garden of Eden.
10. False, this phrase does not appear anywhere in the Bible.
11. False, 1 Timothy 6:10 says, "For *the love of* money is the root of all evil."
12. False, "To thine own self be true" was written by Shakespeare in act 1 of *Hamlet*.
13. False, "Love the sinner, hate the sin" does not appear in the Bible. St. Augustine wrote it in a letter in the fifth century AD.
14. False, according to Matthew 2:11, by the time the wise men visited Jesus, he was in a "house."
15. False, there were two sets. Moses broke one set in anger when he saw the false idol, the golden calf (Exodus 32:19; 34:1).

I hope you scored well on your first test. Simply knowing that these fifteen "facts" are all false puts you ahead of the vast majority of the public. You are well on your way to becoming Bible brilliant.

2. The Essentials

1. "In the beginning God created the heaven and the earth" (Genesis 1:1)
2. Mary (Matthew 1:18)
3. Garden of Eden (Genesis 2:8)
4. Serpent (Genesis 3:1–6)
5. Crucifixion (Mark 15:24–25)
6. Death (Romans 6:23)
7. Aaron (Exodus 7:1)
8. Murder (Genesis 4:8)
9. Daniel (Daniel 6:16)
10. God (Genesis 1:27)
11. "Our Father which art in heaven" (Matthew 6:9)
12. Loaves of bread and fishes (Matthew 14:15–20)
13. Rib (Genesis 2:21–22)
14. Blasphemy against the Holy Ghost (Matthew 12:31; Mark 3:29)
15. Dust (Genesis 2:7)
16. Flood (Genesis 7:7)
17. Peter (Matthew 26:69–74)
18. Crown of thorns (Matthew 27:29)
19. Cain (Genesis 4:9)
20. Stone (Exodus 34:1; Deuteronomy 5:22)
21. Twelve (Luke 6:13)
22. Shepherds (Luke 2:8–17)
23. Exodus
24. Shepherd (1 Samuel 17:12–15)
25. Genesis
26. Matthew
27. He struck him with a stone from his sling (1 Samuel 17:48–50)
28. Judaea (Matthew 3:1)
29. This is Jesus the King of the Jews (Matthew 27:37)
30. Manger (Luke 2:7)
31. Abraham (James 2:21–22)
32. She was a virgin (Matthew 1:22–25)
33. Forty (Genesis 7:12)
34. Moses (Exodus 2:3)
35. He was swallowed by a great fish (Jonah 1:17)
36. She was Naomi's daughter-in-law (Ruth 1:4)
37. Joseph (Matthew 1:18–19)
38. Psalms
39. Swine (Matthew 8:32)
40. Psalm 23 (Psalm 23:1)
41. Paul (Romans 1:1–Jude 1:25)
42. They tossed him into a pit and eventually sold him to strangers (Genesis 37:23–28)
43. Jesse (1 Samuel 17:12; Ruth 4:17, 22)
44. David (Matthew 1:6)
45. Revelation
46. Amen (Revelation 22:21)
47. Sixty-six
48. He washed their feet (John 13:1–5)
49. Cain (Genesis 4:1)
50. Six days (Exodus 20:11)

3. Books of the Bible

1.
   2. Exodus
   4. Numbers
2.
   1. Genesis
   5. Deuteronomy
3.
   3. Leviticus
   5. Deuteronomy
4.
   2. Exodus
   3. Leviticus
5.
   4. Numbers
   6. Joshua
6.
   5. Deuteronomy
   7. Judges
   8. Ruth

7.
  7. Judges
  9. 1 Samuel
8.
  5. Deuteronomy
  8. Ruth
  10. 2 Samuel
9.
  6. Joshua
  8. Ruth
10.
  8. Ruth
  10. 2 Samuel
  12. 2 Kings
11.
  9. 1 Samuel
  11. 1 Kings
  13. 1 Chronicles
12.
  10. 2 Samuel
  12. 2 Kings
13.
  8. Ruth
  11. 1 Kings
  13. 1 Chronicles
14.
  12. 2 Kings
  15. Ezra
  18. Job
15.
  15. Ezra
  17. Esther
  19. Psalms
16.
  16. Nehemiah
  20. Proverbs
17.
  15. Ezra
  18. Job
  20. Proverbs
18.
  12. 2 Kings
  15. Ezra
  17. Esther
  20. Proverbs

19.
  11. 1 Kings
  16. Nehemiah
  19. Psalms
20.
  17. Esther
  20. Proverbs
  22. Song of Solomon
21.
  19. Psalms
  21. Ecclesiastes
  23. Isaiah
22.
  17. Esther
  21. Ecclesiastes
  24. Jeremiah
23.
  18. Job
  22. Song of Solomon
  25. Lamentations
24.
  20. Proverbs
  22. Song of Solomon
  26. Ezekiel
  29. Joel
25.
  22. Song of Solomon
  25. Lamentations
  30. Amos
26.
  23. Isaiah
  26. Ezekiel
  28. Hosea
27.
  20. Proverbs
  24. Jeremiah
  27. Daniel
  30. Amos
28.
  22. Song of Solomon
  25. Lamentations
  29. Joel
29.
  23. Isaiah
  26. Ezekiel
  27. Daniel
  29. Joel

30.
  20. Proverbs
  24. Jeremiah
  27. Daniel
  30. Amos
31.
  26. Ezekiel
  29. Joel
  32. Jonah
  34. Nahum
32.
  28. Hosea
  31. Obadiah
  33. Micah
33.
  26. Ezekiel
  31. Obadiah
  34. Nahum
34.
  27. Daniel
  32. Jonah
  35. Habakkuk
35.
  32. Jonah
  35. Habakkuk
  37. Haggai
36.
  33. Micah
  36. Zephaniah
  39. Malachi
37.
  31. Obadiah
  34. Nahum
  37. Haggai
  39. Malachi
38.
  32. Jonah
  35. Habakkuk
  37. Haggai
39.
  30. Amos
  33. Micah
  36. Zephaniah
  38. Zechariah
40.
  42. Luke

41.
40. Matthew
43. John
42.
41. Mark
44. Acts
43.
41. Mark
43. John
45. Romans
46. 1 Corinthians
47. 2 Corinthians
49. Ephesians
44.
44. Acts
47. 2 Corinthians
50. Philippians
45.
43. John
44. Acts
46. 1 Corinthians
48. Galatians
46.
45. Romans
48. Galatians
51. Colossians
53. 2 Thessalonians
47.
47. 2 Corinthians
49. Ephesians
51. Colossians
55. 2 Timothy

48.
50. Philippians
52. 1 Thessalonians
49.
49. Ephesians
51. Colossians
56. Titus
58. Hebrews
50.
50. Philippians
53. 2 Thessalonians
57. Philemon
59. James
51.
49. Ephesians
54. 1 Timothy
55. 2 Timothy
57. Philemon
59. James
52.
50. Philippians
51. Colossians
56. Titus
59. James
53.
53. 2 Thessalonians
57. Philemon
60. 1 Peter
54.
53. 2 Thessalonians
55. 2 Timothy
58. Hebrews

55.
59. James
62. 1 John
56.
55. 2 Timothy
56. Titus
60. 1 Peter
62. 1 John
57.
61. 2 Peter
64. 3 John
58.
58. Hebrews
60. 1 Peter
62. 1 John
64. 3 John
59.
59. James
65. Jude
60.
56. Titus
58. Hebrews
61. 2 Peter
64. 3 John
66. Revelation

5. 150 Key Verses

1. believeth
2. Word
3. Father
4. nations
5. sinned
6. grace
7. beginning
8. power
9. All
10. Jesus

11. death
12. Repent
13. believe
14. good
15. Light
16. image
17. bodies
18. sinners
19. power
20. born

21. gospel
22. thief
23. Word
24. salvation
25. prayers
26. Spirit
27. Trust
28. evil
29. saved
30. world

31. troubled
32. baptized
33. evangelists
34. sin
35. rest
36. faith
37. created
38. gospel
39. cleanse
40. Pentecost
41. Christ
42. faith
43. approved
44. condemnation
45. saved
46. free
47. government
48. love
49. one
50. commandment
51. truth
52. Christ
53. sins
54. Father
55. darkness
56. spirit
57. Confess
58. virgin
59. believe
60. water
61. mind
62. sin
63. wrath
64. nothing
65. witnesses
66. made
67. rock
68. crucified
69. throne
70. fulfil

71. faith
72. righteousness
73. Spirit
74. truth
75. blood
76. salvation
77. truth
78. power
79. God
80. tables
81. baptized
82. righteous
83. woman
84. faith
85. Father
86. death
87. spirit
88. kind
89. joy
90. firstborn
91. mind
92. hope
93. praise
94. cloud
95. Samaria
96. humbly
97. Sanctify
98. Paul
99. house
100. resurrection
101. Abraham
102. tongues
103. branches
104. baptized
105. child
106. serpent
107. wisdom
108. prophets
109. truth's
110. eternal

111. water
112. disciples
113. instructed
114. voice
115. tasted
116. Father
117. hope
118. will
119. begotten
120. Abram
121. Spirit
122. vine
123. life
124. Let
125. light
126. chosen
127. sixth
128. judgment
129. Rabbi
130. light
131. Moses
132. deceived
133. life
134. Ask
135. Blessed
136. birth
137. excuse
138. Jesus
139. light
140. hope
141. forsake
142. spirit
143. gift
144. treasures
145. preach
146. one
147. promise
148. Jesus
149. sick
150. Son

6. Maintaining Budgets

1. Proverbs 6:6–8

   Go to the ant, thou <u>sluggard</u>;
   consider her ways, and be
   wise: Which having no <u>guide</u>,
   overseer, or ruler, Provideth
   her meat in the summer, and
   gathereth her food in the
   <u>harvest</u>.

2. Proverbs 21:5

   The <u>thoughts</u> of the <u>diligent</u>
   tend only to plenteousness; but
   of every one that is <u>hasty</u> only
   to want.

3. Proverbs 22:3

   A prudent man <u>foreseeth</u> the
   evil, and <u>hideth</u> himself: but
   the <u>simple</u> pass on, and are
   <u>punished</u>.

4. Proverbs 24:3–4

   Through <u>wisdom</u> is an house
   builded; and by understanding
   it is established: And by
   <u>knowledge</u> shall the <u>chambers</u>
   be <u>filled</u> with all precious and
   <u>pleasant</u> riches.

5. Proverbs 25:28

   He that hath no <u>rule</u> over his
   own <u>spirit</u> is like a <u>city</u> that is
   broken down, and without <u>walls</u>.

6. Proverbs 27:12

   A <u>prudent</u> man foreseeth the
   <u>evil</u>, and hideth <u>himself</u>; but
   the simple <u>pass</u> on, and are
   punished.

7. Proverbs 27:23

   Be thou <u>diligent</u> to know the
   state of thy <u>flocks</u>, and <u>look</u> well
   to thy <u>herds</u>.

8. Proverbs 27:26

   The <u>lambs</u> are for thy <u>clothing</u>,
   and the goats are the <u>price</u> of
   the <u>field</u>.

9. Luke 14:28–30

   For which of you, intending to
   <u>build</u> a <u>tower</u>, sitteth not down
   first, and counteth the cost,
   whether he have sufficient
   to <u>finish</u> it? Lest haply, after
   he hath laid the <u>foundation</u>,
   and is not able to finish it, all
   that behold it begin to <u>mock</u>
   him, Saying, This man began
   to build, and was not able to
   finish.

10. 1 Corinthians 16:2

    Upon the first day of the <u>week</u>
    let every one of you <u>lay</u> by him
    in store, as God hath <u>prospered</u>
    him, that there be no <u>gatherings</u>
    when I come.

7. Debt

1. Exodus 22:14

   And if a man <u>borrow</u> ought of
   his neighbour, and it be <u>hurt</u>,
   or <u>die</u>, the owner thereof being
   not with it, he shall surely make
   it <u>good</u>.

2. Deuteronomy 15:6

   For the Lord thy God blesseth
   thee, as he <u>promised</u> thee:
   and thou shalt lend unto many
   <u>nations</u>, but thou shalt not
   <u>borrow</u>; and thou shalt <u>reign</u>
   over many nations, but they
   shall not reign over thee.

3. Deuteronomy 28:12

The LORD shall open unto thee his good <u>treasure</u>, the <u>heaven</u> to give the rain unto thy land in his <u>season</u>, and to bless all the work of thine <u>hand</u>: and thou shalt lend unto many <u>nations</u>, and thou shalt not borrow.

4. 2 Kings 4:7

Then she came and told the man of <u>God</u>. And he said, Go, sell the <u>oil</u>, and pay thy <u>debt</u>, and live thou and thy <u>children</u> of the rest.

5. Psalm 37:21

The wicked borroweth, and <u>payeth</u> not again: but the <u>righteous</u> sheweth <u>mercy</u>, and giveth.

6. Proverbs 22:7

The <u>rich</u> ruleth over the <u>poor</u>, and the <u>borrower</u> is servant to the <u>lender</u>.

7. Proverbs 22:26–27

Be not thou one of them that strike <u>hands</u>, or of them that are <u>sureties</u> for <u>debts</u>. If thou hast <u>nothing</u> to pay, why should he take away thy <u>bed</u> from under thee?

8. Ecclesiastes 5:5

<u>Better</u> is it that thou shouldest not <u>vow</u>, than that thou shouldest vow and not <u>pay</u>.

9. Romans 13:8

Owe no <u>man</u> any thing, but to love one <u>another</u>: for he that loveth another hath fulfilled the <u>law</u>.

8. Wealth

1. Exodus 23:12

Six days thou shalt do thy work, and on the <u>seventh</u> day thou shalt rest: that thine <u>ox</u> and thine ass may rest, and the son of thy <u>handmaid</u>, and the <u>stranger</u>, may be <u>refreshed</u>.

2. Proverbs 12:11

He that tilleth his <u>land</u> shall be satisfied with <u>bread</u>: but he that followeth <u>vain</u> persons is <u>void</u> of understanding.

3. Proverbs 13:11

<u>Wealth</u> gotten by <u>vanity</u> shall be <u>diminished</u>: but he that gathereth by labour shall <u>increase</u>.

4. Proverbs 14:15

The <u>simple</u> believeth every <u>word</u>: but the prudent <u>man</u> looketh <u>well</u> to his going.

5. Proverbs 19:2

Also, that the soul be without <u>knowledge</u>, it is not <u>good</u>; and he that hasteth with his <u>feet</u> <u>sinneth</u>.

6. Proverbs 21:5

The <u>thoughts</u> of the <u>diligent</u> <u>tend</u> only to plenteousness; but of <u>every</u> one that is <u>hasty</u> only to want.

7. Proverbs 23:4

<u>Labour</u> not to be <u>rich</u>: cease from <u>thine</u> own <u>wisdom</u>.

8. Proverbs 28:19–20

He that tilleth his land shall have plenty of <u>bread</u>: but he that followeth after <u>vain</u> persons shall have <u>poverty</u> enough. A faithful man shall abound with blessings: but he that maketh haste to be <u>rich</u> shall not be <u>innocent</u>.

10. Being Happy with What You Have

1. Psalm 23:1

The LORD is my <u>shepherd</u>; I shall not <u>want</u>.

2. Ecclesiastes 5:10

He that loveth <u>silver</u> shall not be satisfied with silver; nor he that loveth <u>abundance</u> with <u>increase</u>: this is also <u>vanity</u>.

3. Matthew 6:31–33

Therefore take no <u>thought</u>, saying, What shall we eat? or, What shall we <u>drink</u>? or, Wherewithal shall we be <u>clothed</u>? (For after all these things do the <u>Gentiles</u> seek:) for your heavenly Father knoweth that ye have need of all these things. But seek ye first the kingdom of God, and his <u>righteousness</u>; and all these things shall be added unto you.

4. Luke 3:14

And the <u>soldiers</u> likewise demanded of him, saying, And what shall we do? And he said unto them, Do <u>violence</u> to no man, neither accuse any <u>falsely</u>; and be content with your <u>wages</u>.

5. Philippians 4:11–13

Not that I speak in respect of want: for I have learned, in whatsoever <u>state</u> I am, therewith to be <u>content</u>. I know both how to be abased, and I know how to abound: every where and in all things I am <u>instructed</u> both to be full and to be <u>hungry</u>, both to abound and to suffer need. I can do all things through <u>Christ</u> which strengtheneth me.

6. 1 Thessalonians 4:11

And that ye study to be <u>quiet</u>, and to do your own <u>business</u>, and to work with your own <u>hands</u>, as we <u>commanded</u> you.

7. 1 Timothy 6:6

But <u>godliness</u> with <u>contentment</u> is great <u>gain</u>.

8. 1 Timothy 6:7–10

For we brought nothing into this world, and it is certain we can carry nothing out. And having food and <u>raiment</u> let us be therewith content. But they that will be rich fall into temptation and a snare, and into many <u>foolish</u> and hurtful <u>lusts</u>, which drown men in <u>destruction</u> and perdition. For the love of money is the root of all evil: which while some coveted after, they have erred from the <u>faith</u>, and pierced themselves through with many <u>sorrows</u>.

9. Hebrews 13:5

Let your <u>conversation</u> be without covetousness; and be content with such things as ye have: for he hath said, I will <u>never</u> leave thee, nor <u>forsake</u> thee.

10. James 4:1–3

From whence come <u>wars</u> and fightings among you? come they not hence, even of your lusts that <u>war</u> in your <u>members</u>? Ye lust, and have not: ye kill, and desire to have, and cannot obtain: ye fight and war, yet ye have not, because ye ask not. Ye <u>ask</u>, and receive not, because ye ask amiss, that ye may <u>consume</u> it upon your lusts.

11. Giving and Being Generous

1. Deuteronomy 15:10

Thou shalt surely give him, and thine <u>heart</u> shall not be grieved when thou givest unto him: because that for this thing the Lᴏʀᴅ thy God shall <u>bless</u> thee in all thy <u>works</u>, and in all that thou puttest thine <u>hand</u> unto.

2. Deuteronomy 16:17

Every <u>man</u> shall give as he is able, according to the <u>blessing</u> of the Lᴏʀᴅ thy <u>God</u> which he hath given <u>thee</u>.

3. 1 Chronicles 29:9

Then the <u>people</u> rejoiced, for that they offered willingly, because with perfect <u>heart</u> they offered willingly to the Lᴏʀᴅ: and <u>David</u> the <u>king</u> also rejoiced with great joy.

4. Proverbs 3:9–10

Honour the Lᴏʀᴅ with thy <u>substance</u>, and with the <u>firstfruits</u> of all thine increase: So shall thy <u>barns</u> be filled with plenty, and thy <u>presses</u> shall burst out with new <u>wine</u>.

5. Proverbs 3:27

Withhold not <u>good</u> from them to whom it is <u>due</u>, when it is in the <u>power</u> of thine <u>hand</u> to do it.

6. Proverbs 11:24–25

There is that <u>scattereth</u>, and yet <u>increaseth</u>; and there is that withholdeth more than is meet, but it tendeth to poverty. The liberal <u>soul</u> shall be made <u>fat</u>: and he that watereth shall be <u>watered</u> also himself.

7. Proverbs 21:26

He <u>coveteth</u> <u>greedily</u> all the <u>day</u> long: but the righteous giveth and <u>spareth</u> not.

8. Proverbs 22:9

He that hath a bountiful <u>eye</u> shall be <u>blessed</u>; for he giveth of his <u>bread</u> to the <u>poor</u>.

9. Proverbs 28:27

He that giveth unto the <u>poor</u> shall not <u>lack</u>: but he that hideth his <u>eyes</u> shall have many a <u>curse</u>.

10. Malachi 3:10

Bring ye all the tithes into the <u>storehouse</u>, that there may be meat in mine house, and prove me now herewith, saith the Lᴏʀᴅ of <u>hosts</u>, if I will not open you the windows of heaven, and pour you out a <u>blessing</u>, that there shall not be <u>room</u> enough to receive it.

11. Matthew 6:3–4

But when thou doest <u>alms</u>, let not thy left <u>hand</u> know what thy right hand doeth: That thine alms may be in <u>secret</u>: and thy <u>Father</u> which seeth in secret himself shall reward <u>thee</u> openly.

12. Mark 12:41–44

And Jesus sat over against the <u>treasury</u>, and beheld how the people <u>cast</u> money into the treasury: and many that were rich cast in much. And there came a certain poor widow, and she threw in two mites, which make a farthing. And he called unto him his disciples, and saith unto them, Verily I say unto you, That this poor widow hath cast more in, than all they which have cast into the treasury: For all they did cast in of their <u>abundance</u>; but she of her want did cast in all that she had, even all her <u>living</u>.

13. Luke 3:11

He <u>answereth</u> and saith unto them, He that hath two <u>coats</u>, let him <u>impart</u> to him that hath <u>none</u>; and he that hath <u>meat</u>, let him do likewise.

14. Luke 6:30

Give to every <u>man</u> that asketh of <u>thee</u>; and of him that taketh away thy <u>goods</u> ask them not again.

15. Luke 6:38

Give, and it shall be given unto you; good measure, pressed down, and <u>shaken</u> together, and <u>running</u> over, shall men give into your <u>bosom</u>. For with the same measure that ye mete withal it shall be <u>measured</u> to you again.

16. Acts 20:35

I have shewed you all <u>things</u>, how that so <u>labouring</u> ye ought to support the weak, and to remember the words of the Lord <u>Jesus</u>, how he said, It is more <u>blessed</u> to give than to receive.

17. Romans 12:8

Or he that exhorteth, on <u>exhortation</u>: he that giveth, let him do it with <u>simplicity</u>; he that ruleth, with <u>diligence</u>; he that sheweth mercy, with <u>cheerfulness</u>.

18. 2 Corinthians 9:6–8

But this I say, He which <u>soweth</u> sparingly shall reap also sparingly; and he which soweth bountifully shall reap also bountifully. Every man according as he purposeth in his <u>heart</u>, so let him give; not <u>grudgingly</u>, or of necessity: for God loveth a cheerful giver. And God is able to make all grace <u>abound</u> toward you; that ye, always having all <u>sufficiency</u> in all things, may abound to every good <u>work</u>.

19. 2 Corinthians 9:10

Now he that ministereth <u>seed</u> to the sower both minister <u>bread</u> for your <u>food</u>, and multiply your seed sown, and increase the <u>fruits</u> of your righteousness.

20. Galatians 6:7

Be not deceived; <u>God</u> is not <u>mocked</u>: for whatsoever a man <u>soweth</u>, that shall he also <u>reap</u>.

21. Philippians 4:15–17

Now ye Philippians know
also, that in the beginning of
the gospel, when I departed
from Macedonia, no church
communicated with me as
concerning giving and receiving,
but ye only. For even in
Thessalonica ye sent once and
again unto my necessity. Not
because I desire a gift: but I
desire fruit that may abound to
your account.

22. James 2:15–16

If a brother or sister be naked,
and destitute of daily food,
And one of you say unto them,
Depart in peace, be ye warmed
and filled; notwithstanding ye
give them not those things
which are needful to the body;
what doth it profit?

12. All about Food

1. C (Matthew 3:4)
2. D (Genesis 25:34)
3. B (Genesis 40)
4. C (Genesis 27)
5. B (Ezekiel 3:3)
6. A (Judges 6:19)
7. B (Exodus 3:17)
8. D (Luke 15:22–24)
9. C (Numbers 11:4–5)
10. D (Judges 14:8–10)
11. B (2 Kings 4:38–41)
12. B (Exodus 16:31)

13. From Sweet to Bitter

1. D (Revelation 10:8–10)
2. C (Judges 14:12–14)
3. A (Proverbs 20:16–18)
4. C (Jeremiah 31:28–30)
5. C (Exodus 12:8)
6. D (Proverbs 9:17)
7. A (Exodus 15:23–25)
8. D (Mark 16:18)
9. D (Exodus 32:20)
10. C (Proverbs 27:7)

14. Residential Area

1. C (Genesis 9:21)
2. D (1 Samuel 17:54)
3. A (Genesis 9:27)
4. B (Joshua 7:20–21)
5. B (Genesis 24:67)
6. A (Genesis 4:20)
7. A (Song of Solomon 1:5)
8. C (Zechariah 12:7)
9. A (Numbers 25:1–8)
10. B (Jeremiah 35:5–7)
11. A (2 Kings 7:3–16)
12. C (Habakkuk 3:7)

15. Kiddie Land

1. A (Genesis 4:1)
2. C (Genesis 9:22–24)
3. B (1 Samuel 16:6–13)
4. B (Genesis 48:13–14)
5. D (1 Kings 16:28–30)
6. B (Genesis 35:16–19)
7. B (Judges 8:30)
8. A (2 Chronicles 11:21)
9. B (1 Corinthians 14:20)
10. C (2 Samuel 17:14–17; 18:33)

17. Window Display

1. A (Acts 20:9)
2. C (Genesis 8:6–8)
3. B (2 Samuel 6:16, 20–21)
4. A (1 Samuel 19:11–12)
5. A (2 Kings 13:16–17)
6. A (Acts 9:1–25)
7. C (Genesis 26:8)
8. D (2 Kings 9:30–37)
9. A (Proverbs 7:6–23)
10. B (Malachi 3:10)

18. That Makes Scents

1. B (Matthew 2:11)
2. D (Esther 2:12–14)
3. C (John 12:3)
4. A (Luke 7:36)
5. C (Song of Solomon 4:13–15)
6. B (Proverbs 7:17)
7. A (Song of Solomon 3:6–7)
8. B (Daniel 10:2–3)
9. B (Proverbs 27:9)
10. D (Jeremiah 4:30; Ezekiel 23:40)

19. Nighty-Night

1. A (Genesis 32:24–32)
2. B (Exodus 12:12)
3. B (1 Samuel 3:1–18)
4. C (Acts 12:5–10)
5. C (Acts 27:1–44)
6. D (John 3:1–2)
7. B (Mark 6:45–51)
8. D (John 18:2–5)
9. A (1 Samuel 26:7–12)
10. C (1 Samuel 28:7–8)
11. B (Judges 7:15–20)

20. Wedding Bells

1. B (Genesis 4:19)
2. D (Genesis 29:1–35)
3. B (1 Samuel 1:1–2)
4. B (1 Samuel 14:50)
5. B (Ruth 4:8–10)
6. D (Genesis 38:1–30)
7. A (2 Chronicles 13:21)
8. A (Judges 14:20)

21. Farming

1. D (Genesis 2:8)
2. B (Job 1:1–22)
3. D (Ecclesiastes 2:4–5)
4. A (Judges 6:11)
5. D (Genesis 9:20)
6. C (Ruth 1:22–2:3; 4:13–17)
7. B (Genesis 26:12)
8. A (2 Chronicles 26:9–10)
9. B (1 Kings 21:1–4)
10. C (2 Samuel 9:1–13)

22. Fill in the Blanks

1. Genesis 1:1
   In the <u>beginning</u> God created the <u>heaven</u> and the <u>earth</u>.

2. Psalm 37:4
   Delight <u>thyself</u> also in the L<small>ORD</small>: and he shall give thee the <u>desires</u> of thine <u>heart</u>.

3. Isaiah 9:6

For unto us a <u>child</u> is born,
unto us a son is given: and the
<u>government</u> shall be upon his
shoulder: and his name shall
be called <u>Wonderful</u>, Counsellor,
The mighty God, The everlasting
Father, The Prince of Peace.

4. Isaiah 40:28

Hast thou not <u>known</u>? hast thou
not heard, that the <u>everlasting</u>
God, the LORD, the Creator
of the ends of the earth,
fainteth not, neither is <u>weary</u>?
there is no searching of his
understanding.

5. Jeremiah 29:11

For I know the <u>thoughts</u> that I
think toward you, saith the LORD,
thoughts of peace, and not of
<u>evil</u>, to give you an expected end.

6. John 3:16

For God so <u>loved</u> the <u>world</u>, that
he gave his only begotten <u>Son</u>,
that whosoever believeth in
him should not perish, but have
everlasting <u>life</u>.

7. John 15:7

If ye <u>abide</u> in me, and my words
abide in you, ye shall ask what
ye <u>will</u>, and it shall be done
unto <u>you</u>.

8. Romans 4:21

And being <u>fully</u> persuaded that,
what he had <u>promised</u>, he was
able also to <u>perform</u>.

9. Romans 8:1

There is therefore now no
<u>condemnation</u> to them which
are in Christ <u>Jesus</u>, who walk
not after the flesh, but after the
<u>Spirit</u>.

10. Romans 8:28

And we know that all things
<u>work</u> together for <u>good</u> to them
that <u>love</u> God, to them who
are the called according to his
<u>purpose</u>.

11. 2 Corinthians 1:20

For all the <u>promises</u> of God in
him are yea, and in him <u>Amen</u>,
unto the <u>glory</u> of God by us.

12. Ephesians 2:10

For we are his workmanship,
created in Christ Jesus unto
good <u>works</u>, which God hath
before <u>ordained</u> that we should
walk in them.

13. Philippians 4:6–7

Be careful for <u>nothing</u>; but
in every thing by <u>prayer</u> and
supplication with <u>thanksgiving</u>
let your requests be made
known unto God. And the
peace of God, which passeth
all understanding, shall keep
your hearts and <u>minds</u> through
Christ Jesus.

14. Philippians 4:19

But my God shall <u>supply</u> all your
need according to his <u>riches</u> in
<u>glory</u> by Christ Jesus.

15. 2 Peter 1:4

Whereby are given unto us
exceeding <u>great</u> and precious
<u>promises</u>: that by these ye
might be partakers of the divine
<u>nature</u>, having escaped the
corruption that is in the world
through lust.

23. Scriptures on Salvation

1. John 14:6
   Jesus saith unto him, I am the way, the truth, and the life: no man cometh unto the Father, but by me.

2. Romans 3:23
   For all have sinned, and come short of the glory of God.

3. Romans 6:23
   For the wages of sin is death; but the gift of God is eternal life through Jesus Christ our Lord.

4. 2 Corinthians 5:17
   Therefore if any man be in Christ, he is a new creature: old things are passed away; behold, all things are become new.

5. Ephesians 2:8–9
   For by grace are ye saved through faith; and that not of yourselves: it is the gift of God: Not of works, lest any man should boast.

6. Revelation 3:20
   Behold, I stand at the door, and knock: if any man hear my voice, and open the door, I will come in to him, and will sup with him, and he with me.

24. Scriptures on Security

1. Psalm 27:1
   The LORD is my light and my salvation; whom shall I fear? the LORD is the strength of my life; of whom shall I be afraid?

2. Psalm 37:4
   Delight thyself also in the LORD: and he shall give thee the desires of thine heart.

3. Proverbs 3:5–6
   Trust in the LORD with all thine heart; and lean not unto thine own understanding. In all thy ways acknowledge him, and he shall direct thy paths.

4. Isaiah 40:31
   But they that wait upon the LORD shall renew their strength; they shall mount up with wings as eagles; they shall run, and not be weary; and they shall walk, and not faint.

5. Jeremiah 29:11
   For I know the thoughts that I think toward you, saith the LORD, thoughts of peace, and not of evil, to give you an expected end.

6. Lamentations 3:22–23
   It is of the LORD'S mercies that we are not consumed, because his compassions fail not. They are new every morning: great is thy faithfulness.

7. Matthew 11:28–30
   Come unto me, all ye that labour and are heavy laden, and I will give you rest. Take my yoke upon you, and learn of me; for I am meek and lowly in heart: and ye shall find rest unto your souls. For my yoke is easy, and my burden is light.

8. Luke 16:13

No <u>servant</u> can serve two <u>masters</u>: for either he will hate the one, and love the other; or else he will hold to the one, and despise the other. Ye cannot serve <u>God</u> and mammon.

9. Acts 1:8

But ye shall receive <u>power</u>, after that the Holy <u>Ghost</u> is come upon you: and ye shall be witnesses unto me both in <u>Jerusalem</u>, and in all Judaea, and in Samaria, and unto the uttermost part of the <u>earth</u>.

10. Romans 8:28

And we know that all <u>things</u> work together for <u>good</u> to them that love God, to them who are the called according to his <u>purpose</u>.

11. Romans 8:38–39

For I am persuaded, that neither <u>death</u>, nor life, nor <u>angels</u>, nor principalities, nor powers, nor things present, nor things to come, Nor <u>height</u>, nor depth, nor any other creature, shall be able to separate us from the love of God, which is in Christ Jesus our <u>Lord</u>.

12. Romans 12:1

I beseech you therefore, <u>brethren</u>, by the mercies of <u>God</u>, that ye present your bodies a living <u>sacrifice</u>, holy, acceptable unto God, which is your reasonable <u>service</u>.

13. 1 Corinthians 15:58

Therefore, my beloved brethren, be ye stedfast, <u>unmoveable</u>, always abounding in the <u>work</u> of the Lord, forasmuch as ye know

that your labour is not in <u>vain</u> in the Lord.

14. 2 Corinthians 4:18

While we <u>look</u> not at the things which are <u>seen</u>, but at the things which are not seen: for the things which are seen are <u>temporal</u>; but the things which are not seen are <u>eternal</u>.

15. 2 Corinthians 12:9

And he said unto me, My <u>grace</u> is sufficient for <u>thee</u>: for my strength is made perfect in weakness. Most gladly therefore will I rather glory in my <u>infirmities</u>, that the power of Christ may rest upon me.

16. Galatians 2:20

I am <u>crucified</u> with Christ: nevertheless I live; yet not I, but Christ liveth in me: and the <u>life</u> which I now live in the flesh I live by the <u>faith</u> of the Son of God, who loved me, and gave himself for me.

17. Galatians 5:22–23

But the <u>fruit</u> of the Spirit is love, joy, peace, <u>longsuffering</u>, gentleness, goodness, <u>faith</u>, Meekness, temperance: against such there is no law.

18. Philippians 4:13

I can do all <u>things</u> through Christ which <u>strengtheneth</u> me.

19. Colossians 3:23

And whatsoever ye do, do it <u>heartily</u>, as to the Lord, and not unto <u>men</u>.

20. Hebrews 12:1–2

Wherefore seeing we also are compassed about with so great a cloud of <u>witnesses</u>, let us lay aside every <u>weight</u>, and the sin which doth so easily beset us, and let us run with patience the race that is set before us, looking unto Jesus the author and finisher of our <u>faith</u>; who for the joy that was set before him endured the <u>cross</u>, despising the shame, and is set down at the right hand of the throne of God.

21. Hebrews 13:8

Jesus Christ the same <u>yesterday</u>, and to day, and for <u>ever</u>.

22. James 1:22

But be ye <u>doers</u> of the <u>word</u>, and not hearers only, deceiving your own <u>selves</u>.

23. James 4:7

<u>Submit</u> yourselves therefore to <u>God</u>. Resist the devil, and he will <u>flee</u> from you.

24. 2 Peter 3:9

The <u>Lord</u> is not slack concerning his <u>promise</u>, as some men count slackness; but is longsuffering to us-ward, not willing that any should <u>perish</u>, but that all should come to repentance.

25. 1 John 4:7–8

Beloved, let us <u>love</u> one another: for love is of God; and every one that loveth is born of God, and knoweth <u>God</u>. He that loveth not knoweth not God; for God is love.

25. Crossword Puzzle 1

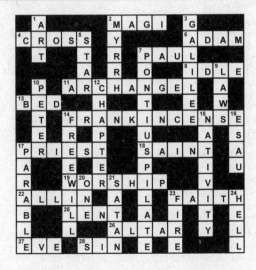

SECTION 2: THE ADVANCED SECTION

26. Group 1

1. True—(1 Chronicles 1:34)
2. False—Amnon was David's firstborn son (1 Chronicles 3:1)
3. False—Rehoboam was king after him (1 Chronicles 3:10)
4. False—Her hair is her glory (1 Corinthians 11:15)
5. True—(1 Corinthians 15:50)
6. True—(1 Corinthians 15:56)
7. True—(1 Corinthians 6:19)
8. False—He refers to himself as an apostle (1 Corinthians 9:1)
9. False—Solomon would be king (1 Kings 1:13)
10. False—He ruled for seventeen years (1 Kings 14:21)
11. True—(1 Kings 16:30–31)
12. True—(1 Kings 16:32)
13. False—Elijah performed the miracle (1 Kings 17:19–22)
14. True—(1 Kings 17:2–7)
15. False—He met the prophets of Baal on Mount Carmel (1 Kings 18:19)
16. True—(1 Kings 18:46)
17. False—He was fed two meals (1 Kings 19:5–8)
18. True—(1 Kings 19:8)
19. True—(1 Kings 19:8)
20. True—(1 Kings 4:26)

27. Group 2

1. False—Benaiah was the commander (1 Kings 4:4)
2. False—He was not allowed to build it (1 Kings 5:3)
3. False—He began to build in the fourth year of his reign (1 Kings 6:1)
4. True—(Ephesians 2:20)
5. True—(1 Peter 5:8)
6. True—(1 Samuel 1:9–20)
7. True—(1 Samuel 9:27; 10:1)
8. False—The head is usually anointed (1 Samuel 10:1)
9. True—(1 Samuel 13:8–14)
10. True—(1 Samuel 16:1, 13)
11. True—(1 Samuel 16:15–19)
12. False—He killed a bear and a lion (1 Samuel 17:34–36)
13. True—(Mark 10:46–52)
14. False—He was from Gath (1 Samuel 17:4)
15. True—(1 Samuel 17:4)
16. False—He took five stones (1 Samuel 17:40)
17. False—He used a slingshot and one stone (1 Samuel 17:49–50)
18. True—(1 Samuel 17:54)
19. True—(1 Samuel 18:11)
20. True—(1 Samuel 18:27)

28. Group 3

1. True—(1 Samuel 18:6–7)
2. True—(1 Samuel 2:18–21)
3. True—(1 Samuel 20:16–17)
4. False—He gave David Goliath's sword (1 Samuel 21:8–9)

5. False—He massacred eighty-five priests in the town of Nod (1 Samuel 22:18)
6. True—(1 Samuel 25:3)
7. True—(1 Samuel 28:8)
8. True—(1 Samuel 3:2–10)
9. False—His bones were buried under a tree (1 Samuel 31:12–13)
10. True—(1 Samuel 31:2)
11. True—(1 Samuel 31:3)
12. False—Three of his sons were killed (1 Samuel 31:8)
13. True—(1 Samuel 4:11)
14. True—(1 Samuel 4:4–5)
15. True—(1 Samuel 5:2)
16. True—(1 Samuel 7:17)
17. True—(1 Samuel 7:17)
18. True—(1 Samuel 9:1–2)
19. True—(1 Timothy 2:5)
20. False—Christians should lift up holy hands (1 Timothy 2:8)

29. Group 4

1. True—(2 Chronicles 13:21)
2. True—(2 Chronicles 17:11)
3. False—He saw the Lord sitting upon his throne (2 Chronicles 18:8–18)
4. True—(2 Chronicles 2:8)
5. True—(2 Chronicles 26:9–10)
6. True—(2 Chronicles 26:21)
7. False—Josiah disguised himself (2 Chronicles 35:20–22)
8. False—He was Hebrew by birth (Philippians 3:5)
9. True—(2 Corinthians 11:25)
10. False—Her name appears twice (2 Corinthians 11:3; 1 Timothy 2:13)
11. True—(2 Corinthians 1:1–2; 11:32–33)
12. True—(2 Corinthians 1:1–2; 12:2)
13. False—His bones brought a dead man back to life (2 Kings 13:20–21)
14. True—(2 Kings 2:11)
15. False—It divided (2 Kings 2:12–14)
16. False—He healed the waters of Jericho (2 Kings 2:18–22)
17. True—(Joshua 10:12–13; 2 Kings 20:8–11)
18. True—(2 Kings 22:1)
19. True—(2 Kings 23:29)
20. True—(2 Kings 25:1)

30. Group 5

1. False—Zedekiah was the last king (2 Kings 25:1–7)
2. True—(2 Kings 4:1–12)
3. False—He supplied oil (2 Kings 4:1–7)
4. True—(2 Kings 5:20–27)
5. True—(2 Kings 6:17)
6. True—(2 Kings 8:7–15)
7. True—(Jeremiah 26:20–23)
8. True—(2 Kings 9:31–33)
9. False—Dogs ate her body (2 Kings 9:35–37)
10. True—(2 Samuel 11:2–4)
11. True—(2 Samuel 12:1–15)
12. False—Solomon was their second son (2 Samuel 12:24)
13. True—(2 Samuel 12:24–25)
14. True—(2 Samuel 13:37–38)
15. False—He was handsome (2 Samuel 14:25)
16. True—(2 Samuel 15:30)

17. True—(2 Samuel 18:14–17)
18. True—(2 Samuel 2:4)
19. True—(2 Samuel 2:8–9)

20. False—He was also known as Eshbaal (1 Chronicles 9:39)

31. Group 6

1. True—(2 Samuel 20:15–22)
2. True—(2 Samuel 20:9–10)
3. True—(2 Samuel 21:12–14)
4. True—(2 Samuel 4:4)
5. True—(2 Samuel 4:6)
6. False—Jebusites inhabited Jerusalem (2 Samuel 5:6)
7. True—(2 Samuel 6:16)
8. False—Joab was the commander (2 Samuel 8:16)
9. False—His grandmother was Lois (2 Timothy 1:5)
10. False—His mother was Eunice (2 Timothy 1:5)
11. True—(2 Timothy 4:12)
12. False—There were only two soldiers (Acts 12:6)
13. True—(Acts 1:15–26)
14. True—(Acts 10:1–45)
15. True—(Acts 10:24–48)
16. False—They were first called Christians at the church of Antioch (Acts 11:26)
17. True—(Acts 11:27–28)
18. False—James the brother of John was the first (Acts 12:1–2)
19. True—(Acts 12:1–2)
20. True—(Acts 12:18–19)

32. Group 7

1. True—(Acts 12:23)
2. True—(Acts 12:6–17)
3. True—(Acts 13:13–14)
4. True—(Acts 13:9)
5. True—(Acts 14:8–19)
6. True—(Acts 15:32)
7. False—He was accompanied by Silas (Acts 15:40–41)
8. True—(Acts 16:14)
9. True—(Acts 16:14)
10. True—(Acts 16:14–15)
11. False—They were famous for searching the Scriptures (Acts 17:10–11)
12. True—(Acts 18:2)
13. True—(Acts 18:8)
14. True—(Acts 19:19)
15. False—It was in Ephesus (Acts 19:1–9)
16. False—Peter preached at Pentecost (Acts 2)
17. False—He was in Troas (Acts 20:6–9)
18. True—(Acts 9:36–43; 20:9–12)
19. True—(Acts 21:39)
20. True—(Acts 22:3)

33. Group 8

1. True—(Acts 22:3)
2. False—He came to report a conspiracy (Acts 23:16)
3. True—(Acts 23:20–21)
4. True—(Acts 24:1)
5. True—(Acts 24:27)
6. False—He left Paul bound in prison (Acts 24:27)
7. False—It was the name of a storm (Acts 27:14)
8. True—(Acts 28:3–6)

9. False—John and Peter healed a crippled man (Acts 3:1–10)
10. True—(Acts 4:36)
11. False—It means "the son of consolation" (Acts 4:36)
12. False—Joses was his original name (Acts 4:36)
13. False—About five thousand men believed (Acts 4:4)
14. False—A Pharisee was a doctor of the law (Acts 5:34)
15. True—(Acts 5:34)
16. True—(Acts 6:7–8:2)
17. True—(Acts 7:59)
18. False—The Spirit of the Lord carried him (Acts 8:39–40)
19. False—Simon the sorcerer tried to buy the gifts (Acts 8:9, 18–19)
20. False—Saul was headed to Damascus (Acts 9:1)

34. Group 9

1. False—He was healed by Peter (Acts 9:32–34)
2. False—Peter raised her from the dead (Acts 9:36–41)
3. True—(Acts 9:8)
4. False—He was a herdsman (Amos 1:1)
5. False—He spoke about justice rolling down like a river (Amos 5:24)
6. False—He told believers to set their affections on things above (Colossians 3:2)
7. False—He described him as a beloved physician (Colossians 4:14)
8. False—He was king of Babylon (Daniel 1:1)
9. False—It was Mishael (Daniel 1:7)
10. True—(Daniel 2:1)
11. True—(Daniel 2:6)
12. True—(Daniel 5)
13. False—King Darius was "the Mede" (Daniel 5:31)
14. True—(Daniel 6)
15. False—He prayed three times a day (Daniel 6:10)
16. True—(Daniel 6:18)
17. False—He had a vision of a lion with eagle's wings (Daniel 7:4)
18. True—(Daniel 8:15–26; 9:21–27)
19. False—He visited Daniel (Daniel 9:20)
20. False—He was 120 years old (Deuteronomy 34:7)

35. Group 10

1. True—(Deuteronomy 10:6)
2. True—(Deuteronomy 12:6)
3. True—(Deuteronomy 3:11)
4. True—(Deuteronomy 32:48–49)
5. True—(Deuteronomy 34:3)
6. True—(Deuteronomy 34:5–6)
7. False—They mourned for thirty days (Deuteronomy 34:8)
8. True—(Exodus 20:12; Deuteronomy 5:16)
9. True—(Deuteronomy 9:13)
10. True—(Ecclesiastes 2:2)
11. True—(Ephesians 5:14)
12. False—He recommended the Holy Spirit as a substitute for wine (Ephesians 5:18)

13. False—Hadassah was her Hebrew name (Esther 2:7)
14. True—(Esther 2:7)
15. False—He was angry because Mordecai wouldn't bow down to him (Esther 3:5)
16. True—(Esther 3:8–9)
17. False—Zeresh was his wife (Esther 5:10)
18. True—(Exodus 1:13)
19. True—(Exodus 10:16)
20. True—(Exodus 10:19)

37. Memory Verses

1. Genesis 1:1
   In the <u>beginning</u> God created the <u>heaven</u> and the <u>earth</u>.

2. Genesis 1:26
   And God said, Let us make man in our <u>image</u>, after our likeness: and let them have <u>dominion</u> over the fish of the sea, and over the fowl of the air, and over the cattle, and over all the earth, and over every creeping thing that creepeth upon the <u>earth</u>.

3. Genesis 1:27
   So God created man in his own <u>image</u>, in the image of God created he him; <u>male</u> and <u>female</u> created he them.

4. Joshua 1:8
   This book of the law shall not depart out of thy <u>mouth</u>; but thou shalt meditate therein day and <u>night</u>, that thou mayest observe to do according to all that is written therein: for then thou shalt make thy way <u>prosperous</u>, and then thou shalt have good <u>success</u>.

5. Joshua 1:9
   Have not I commanded thee? Be strong and of a good <u>courage</u>; be not afraid, neither be thou <u>dismayed</u>: for the LORD thy God is with <u>thee</u> whithersoever thou goest.

6. Psalm 37:4
   Delight <u>thyself</u> also in the LORD; and he shall give thee the <u>desires</u> of thine <u>heart</u>.

7. Psalm 133:1–2
   Behold, how good and how pleasant it is for <u>brethren</u> to dwell together in <u>unity</u>! It is like the precious <u>ointment</u> upon the head, that ran down upon the <u>beard</u>, even Aaron's beard: that went down to the skirts of his garments.

8. Psalm 139:14
   I will praise thee; for I am <u>fearfully</u> and <u>wonderfully</u> made: marvellous are thy <u>works</u>; and that my soul knoweth right well.

9. Proverbs 3:5–6
   <u>Trust</u> in the LORD with all thine <u>heart</u>; and lean not unto thine own understanding. In all thy ways <u>acknowledge</u> him, and he shall direct thy <u>paths</u>.

10. Proverbs 30:5
    Every <u>word</u> of <u>God</u> is pure: he is a shield unto them that put their <u>trust</u> in him.

11. Isaiah 26:3
    Thou wilt keep him in perfect <u>peace</u>, whose <u>mind</u> is stayed on thee: because he <u>trusteth</u> in thee.

12. Isaiah 40:31

   But they that wait upon the LORD shall renew their <u>strength</u>; they shall mount up with <u>wings</u> as <u>eagles</u>; they shall run, and not be weary; and they shall walk, and not <u>faint</u>.

13. Isaiah 41:10

   Fear thou not; for I am with thee: be not <u>dismayed</u>; for I am thy God: I will strengthen thee; yea, I will help thee; yea, I will uphold <u>thee</u> with the right <u>hand</u> of my righteousness.

14. Isaiah 53:4

   Surely he hath borne our <u>griefs</u>, and carried our sorrows: yet we did esteem him <u>stricken</u>, smitten of God, and <u>afflicted</u>.

15. Isaiah 53:5

   But he was wounded for our <u>transgressions</u>, he was bruised for our <u>iniquities</u>: the <u>chastisement</u> of our peace was upon him; and with his <u>stripes</u> we are healed.

16. Isaiah 53:6

   All we like <u>sheep</u> have gone astray; we have turned every one to his own way; and the LORD hath laid on him the <u>iniquity</u> of us all.

17. Isaiah 55:8

   For my thoughts are not your <u>thoughts</u>, neither are your ways my <u>ways</u>, saith the LORD.

18. Jeremiah 29:11

   For I know the thoughts that I think toward you, saith the LORD, thoughts of <u>peace</u>, and not of <u>evil</u>, to give you an expected <u>end</u>.

19. Micah 6:8

   He hath shewed <u>thee</u>, O man, what is good; and what doth the LORD require of thee, but to do justly, and to love <u>mercy</u>, and to walk <u>humbly</u> with thy God?

20. Matthew 3:2

   And saying, <u>Repent</u> ye: for the <u>kingdom</u> of heaven is at <u>hand</u>.

21. Matthew 5:16

   Let your <u>light</u> so shine before men, that they may see your <u>good</u> works, and glorify your Father which is in <u>heaven</u>.

22. Matthew 11:28–30

   Come unto me, all ye that labour and are heavy laden, and I will give you <u>rest</u>. Take my <u>yoke</u> upon you, and learn of me; for I am <u>meek</u> and lowly in <u>heart</u>: and ye shall find rest unto your souls. For my yoke is easy, and my burden is light.

23. Matthew 22:37

   <u>Jesus</u> said unto him, Thou shalt <u>love</u> the Lord thy God with all thy heart, and with all thy <u>soul</u>, and with all thy <u>mind</u>.

24. Matthew 28:18

   And <u>Jesus</u> came and spake unto them, saying, All <u>power</u> is given unto me in <u>heaven</u> and in <u>earth</u>.

25. Matthew 28:19–20

   Go ye therefore, and teach all <u>nations</u>, baptizing them in the name of the Father, and of the Son, and of the Holy <u>Ghost</u>: Teaching them to <u>observe</u> all things whatsoever I have <u>commanded</u> you: and, lo, I am with you always, even unto the end of the world. Amen.

26. John 1:1

    In the <u>beginning</u> was the <u>Word</u>, and the Word was with God, and the Word was <u>God</u>.

27. John 1:12

    But as many as received him, to them gave he <u>power</u> to become the sons of God, even to them that <u>believe</u> on his <u>name</u>.

28. John 3:16

    For God so loved the <u>world</u>, that he gave his only begotten Son, that whosoever believeth in him should not <u>perish</u>, but have everlasting <u>life</u>.

29. John 3:17

    For God sent not his Son into the <u>world</u> to <u>condemn</u> the world; but that the world through him might be <u>saved</u>.

30. John 5:24

    Verily, verily, I say unto you, He that heareth my <u>word</u>, and believeth on him that sent me, hath everlasting <u>life</u>, and shall not come into condemnation; but is passed from <u>death</u> unto life.

31. John 10:10

    The <u>thief</u> cometh not, but for to steal, and to <u>kill</u>, and to <u>destroy</u>: I am come that they might have <u>life</u>, and that they might have it more abundantly.

32. John 11:25

    Jesus said unto her, I am the <u>resurrection</u>, and the life: he that believeth in me, though he were <u>dead</u>, yet shall he <u>live</u>.

33. John 13:35

    By this shall all <u>men</u> know that ye are my <u>disciples</u>, if ye have <u>love</u> one to another.

34. John 14:6

    <u>Jesus</u> saith unto him, I am the way, the <u>truth</u>, and the <u>life</u>: no man cometh unto the <u>Father</u>, but by me.

35. John 14:27

    Peace I leave with you, my <u>peace</u> I give unto you: not as the <u>world</u> giveth, give I unto you. Let not your <u>heart</u> be troubled, neither let it be afraid.

36. John 15:13

    Greater <u>love</u> hath no <u>man</u> than this, that a man lay down his <u>life</u> for his <u>friends</u>.

37. John 16:33

    These things I have spoken unto you, that in me ye might have <u>peace</u>. In the <u>world</u> ye shall have <u>tribulation</u>: but be of good <u>cheer</u>; I have overcome the world.

38. Acts 1:8

    But ye shall receive <u>power</u>, after that the Holy Ghost is come upon you: and ye shall be <u>witnesses</u> unto me both in <u>Jerusalem</u>, and in all Judaea, and in <u>Samaria</u>, and unto the uttermost part of the <u>earth</u>.

39. Acts 2:38

    Then <u>Peter</u> said unto them, Repent, and be <u>baptized</u> every one of you in the name of Jesus Christ for the remission of <u>sins</u>, and ye shall receive the <u>gift</u> of the Holy Ghost.

40. Acts 4:12

    Neither is there <u>salvation</u> in any other: for there is none other <u>name</u> under heaven given among <u>men</u>, whereby we must be <u>saved</u>.

41. Acts 17:11

These were more noble than those in <u>Thessalonica</u>, in that they received the word with all readiness of <u>mind</u>, and searched the <u>scriptures</u> daily, whether those <u>things</u> were so.

42. Romans 3:23

For all have <u>sinned</u>, and come short of the <u>glory</u> of <u>God</u>.

43. Romans 5:8

But <u>God</u> commendeth his <u>love</u> toward us, in that, while we were yet sinners, <u>Christ</u> died for us.

44. Romans 6:23

For the wages of <u>sin</u> is <u>death</u>; but the gift of God is eternal life through Jesus Christ our <u>Lord</u>.

45. Romans 8:28

And we know that all things <u>work</u> together for good to them that love <u>God</u>, to them who are the called according to his <u>purpose</u>.

46. Romans 8:38–39

For I am persuaded, that neither <u>death</u>, nor life, nor angels, nor principalities, nor <u>powers</u>, nor things present, nor things to come, Nor height, nor depth, nor any other <u>creature</u>, shall be able to separate us from the love of God, which is in Christ Jesus our <u>Lord</u>.

47. Romans 10:9–10

That if thou shalt confess with thy <u>mouth</u> the Lord Jesus, and shalt believe in thine <u>heart</u> that God hath raised him from the <u>dead</u>, thou shalt be saved. For with the heart man believeth unto righteousness; and with the mouth confession is made unto <u>salvation</u>.

48. Romans 10:17

So then <u>faith</u> cometh by <u>hearing</u>, and hearing by the <u>word</u> of God.

49. Romans 12:1

I beseech you therefore, brethren, by the <u>mercies</u> of God, that ye present your <u>bodies</u> a living <u>sacrifice</u>, holy, acceptable unto <u>God</u>, which is your reasonable service.

50. Romans 12:2

And be not <u>conformed</u> to this world: but be ye transformed by the renewing of your <u>mind</u>, that ye may prove what is that good, and <u>acceptable</u>, and perfect, <u>will</u> of God.

51. Romans 15:13

Now the God of <u>hope</u> fill you with all joy and <u>peace</u> in believing, that ye may abound in hope, through the <u>power</u> of the Holy Ghost.

52. 1 Corinthians 6:19

What? know ye not that your <u>body</u> is the temple of the <u>Holy Ghost</u> which is in you, which ye have of God, and ye are not your own?

53. 1 Corinthians 10:13

There hath no temptation taken you but such as is common to man: but God is <u>faithful</u>, who will not <u>suffer</u> you to be tempted above that ye are able; but will with the <u>temptation</u> also make a way to <u>escape</u>, that ye may be able to bear it.

54. 2 Corinthians 5:17

Therefore if any <u>man</u> be in Christ, he is a new <u>creature</u>: old <u>things</u> are passed away; behold, all things are become new.

55. 2 Corinthians 5:21

For he hath made him to be sin for us, who knew no <u>sin</u>; that we might be made the <u>righteousness</u> of God in <u>him</u>.

56. 2 Corinthians 12:9

And he said unto me, My <u>grace</u> is sufficient for thee: for my <u>strength</u> is made perfect in <u>weakness</u>. Most gladly therefore will I rather glory in my <u>infirmities</u>, that the power of Christ may rest upon me.

57. 2 Timothy 1:7

For God hath not given us the <u>spirit</u> of <u>fear</u>; but of <u>power</u>, and of love, and of a sound <u>mind</u>.

58. 2 Timothy 3:16–17

All <u>scripture</u> is given by inspiration of God, and is profitable for <u>doctrine</u>, for reproof, for correction, for <u>instruction</u> in righteousness: That the man of God may be perfect, thoroughly furnished unto all good <u>works</u>.

59. Hebrews 4:12

For the word of God is quick, and powerful, and sharper than any twoedged sword, piercing even to the dividing asunder of <u>soul</u> and <u>spirit</u>, and of the joints and <u>marrow</u>, and is a discerner of the thoughts and intents of the <u>heart</u>.

60. Hebrews 4:15

For we have not an high priest which cannot be <u>touched</u> with the feeling of our <u>infirmities</u>; but was in all points <u>tempted</u> like as we are, yet without sin.

61. Hebrews 4:16

Let us therefore come <u>boldly</u> unto the throne of <u>grace</u>, that we may obtain <u>mercy</u>, and find grace to <u>help</u> in time of need.

62. Hebrews 10:24–25

And let us consider one <u>another</u> to provoke unto <u>love</u> and to good <u>works</u>: Not forsaking the <u>assembling</u> of ourselves together, as the manner of some is; but exhorting one another: and so much the more, as ye see the day approaching.

63. Hebrews 11:1

Now <u>faith</u> is the <u>substance</u> of things hoped for, the <u>evidence</u> of things not seen.

64. Hebrews 11:6

But without <u>faith</u> it is impossible to please him: for he that cometh to God must <u>believe</u> that he is, and that he is a <u>rewarder</u> of them that diligently <u>seek</u> him.

65. Hebrews 12:1–2

Wherefore seeing we also are compassed about with so great a cloud of <u>witnesses</u>, let us lay aside every weight, and the sin which doth so easily beset us, and let us run with patience the race that is set before us, Looking unto Jesus the author and <u>finisher</u> of our faith; who for the joy that was set before him endured the <u>cross</u>, despising the <u>shame</u>, and is set down at the right hand of the throne of God.

66. Hebrews 13:5

Let your <u>conversation</u> be without <u>covetousness</u>; and be <u>content</u> with such things as ye have: for he hath said, I will never leave thee, nor forsake thee.

67. James 1:2–3

My <u>brethren</u>, count it all joy when ye fall into divers <u>temptations</u>; Knowing this, that the trying of your <u>faith</u> worketh patience.

68. James 1:12

<u>Blessed</u> is the man that endureth temptation: for when he is tried, he shall receive the crown of <u>life</u>, which the Lord hath <u>promised</u> to them that <u>love</u> him.

69. James 5:16

Confess your faults one to another, and pray one for another, that ye may be <u>healed</u>. The effectual fervent <u>prayer</u> of a righteous <u>man</u> <u>availeth</u> much.

70. 1 Peter 2:24

Who his own self bare our sins in his own body on the <u>tree</u>, that we, being dead to <u>sins</u>, should live unto <u>righteousness</u>: by whose <u>stripes</u> ye were healed.

71. 1 Peter 3:15–16

But sanctify the Lord God in your <u>hearts</u>: and be ready always to give an answer to every man that asketh you a reason of the hope that is in you with meekness and fear: Having a good <u>conscience</u>; that, whereas they speak evil of you, as of <u>evildoers</u>, they may be ashamed that falsely accuse your good conversation in <u>Christ</u>.

72. 1 Peter 5:7

<u>Casting</u> all your <u>care</u> upon him; for he careth for <u>you</u>.

73. 1 John 1:9

If we confess our <u>sins</u>, he is <u>faithful</u> and just to forgive us our sins, and to cleanse us from all <u>unrighteousness</u>.

74. 1 John 3:16

Hereby perceive we the love of <u>God</u>, because he laid down his <u>life</u> for us: and we ought to lay down our lives for the <u>brethren</u>.

75. Revelation 1:10

I was in the <u>Spirit</u> on the Lord's <u>day</u>, and heard behind me a great <u>voice</u>, as of a <u>trumpet</u>.

38. Names of God Part 1

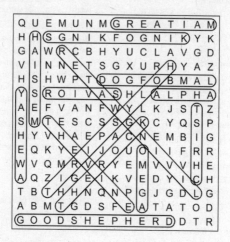

39. Names of God Part 2

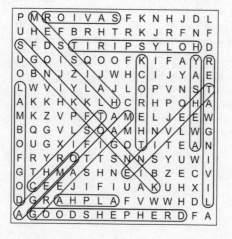

40. Names of God Part 3

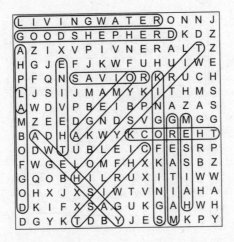

41. People and Angels Part 1

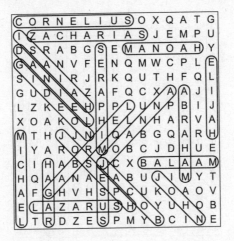

42. People and Angels Part 2

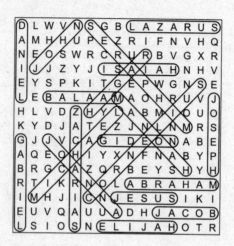

43. People and Angels Part 3

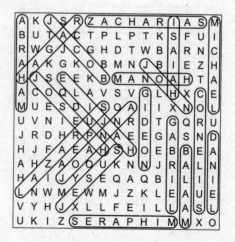

44. The Book of Genesis

Chapter 1

1. Light
2. Firmament (sky)
3. Dry land
4. Stars, sun, and moon
5. Sea animals and flying creatures
6. Beasts of the earth and humans
7. God rested

Chapter 2

1. Dust
2. The ground
3. Adam's rib
4. Garden of Eden

Chapter 3

1. The tree of the knowledge of good and evil
2. The serpent
3. The serpent would have to crawl on his belly and eat dust
4. He would be forced to till the ground in hard labor
5. She would give birth in pain and be subject to man
6. To keep man out of the garden
7. So man would not eat of it and live forever

Chapter 4

1. Because Cain did not honor God with his offering like his brother Abel did
2. Murdered him
3. Put a curse on him
4. Cain was afraid someone would find him and kill him
5. God put a mark on him that identified and protected him
6. Seth

Chapter 5

1. Shem, Ham, and Japheth

Chapter 6

1. They took the daughters of men as wives
2. He viewed it as wicked
3. He was sorry he had made man
4. Noah
5. Build an ark
6. 300 cubits long (450 feet), 50 cubits wide (75 feet), 30 cubits high (45 feet)
7. Two of each

Chapter 7

1. Two of each
2. Seven of each
3. Seven of each
4. Forty
5. Eight
6. They remained in the seas

Chapter 8

1. 150
2. Three
3. First month of the next year

Chapter 9

1. The blood of that man or that beast
2. Rainbow
3. He told his brothers

Chapter 10

1. Ham
2. On the coastlands
3. In the east
4. Noah's sons, Ham, Shem, and Japheth

Chapter 11

1. A tower that would reach to the heavens
2. For fame and so they would not be scattered
3. He gave them many various languages and scattered them
4. 292
5. Abram's nephew (the son of his brother, Haran)

Chapter 12

1. Leave his father's house
2. He would make him a great nation
3. The land of Canaan
4. Because Pharaoh took Abram's wife to his house

Chapter 13

1. There was not enough room for them all
2. They decided to move to separate places
3. Canaan
4. Sodom

Chapter 14

1. Lot
2. Abram
3. Tithed them to God
4. Melchizedek, king of Salem, priest of the most high God
5. To let him keep the spoils of war
6. So the king could not take credit for making Abram rich

Chapter 15

1. One of Abram's servants
2. They would be as numerous as the stars in the heavens
3. They would be held in bondage
4. Four hundred years
5. The land of Canaan

Chapter 16

1. Hagar, her maidservant
2. She hated her
3. He would multiply her descendants
4. Ishmael

Chapter 17

1. Abraham
2. Father of many nations
3. Circumcision
4. Sarah
5. A son

Chapter 18

1. Three men standing by him
2. Angels
3. She would bear him a son
4. She laughed
5. Sodom
6. Lot was in Sodom and would be killed when it was destroyed

Chapter 19

1. Two
2. Lot
3. The men of the city
4. To "know" (have sexual relations with) the "men" in Lot's house
5. Blinded them
6. The Lord
7. Destroy it with brimstone and fire
8. They thought he was joking
9. A small town called Zoar
10. Lot's wife
11. She was turned into a pillar of salt
12. Get him drunk and "lie" (have intercourse) with him
13. To have children since there were no other men around
14. Moabites and Ammonites

Chapter 20

1. He thought someone would kill him to have Sarah for himself
2. God
3. God healed Abimelech, and the women became capable of bearing children

Chapter 21

1. Isaac
2. Laughter
3. Cast them out
4. Make him a nation
5. They would not deal falsely but would show kindness to each other

Chapter 22

1. To test his faith
2. Isaac
3. Because Abraham was about to carry out the sacrifice of his son
4. A ram
5. The seed of Abraham
6. Bethuel

Chapter 23

1. Kirjatharba (or Hebron)
2. In the cave of Machpelah

Chapter 24

1. His oldest servant
2. Rebekah
3. She would offer a drink to him and his camels
4. Covered her face
5. Yes, he loved her

Chapter 25

1. In the cave of Machpelah
2. The twins were two nations
3. Esau and Jacob
4. Hairy and a cunning hunter
5. Esau

6. Because Esau was a hunter and fed Isaac meat
7. His birthright

Chapter 26

1. Gerar
2. His sister
3. King Abimelech
4. Depart from the land
5. Beersheba

Chapter 27

1. Abundance of the land and master over his brethren
2. To live by the sword and faithfully serve his brother
3. Kill him
4. To her brother's house in Haran
5. She did not want Jacob to take his wife from among the daughters of Heth

Chapter 28

1. Laban
2. A ladder going to heaven with angels going up and down it
3. His descendants would be as the dust of the earth
4. Bethel
5. House of God

Chapter 29

1. She was his mother's niece
2. Shepherdess
3. Rachel as his wife
4. Leah
5. Seven years
6. Reuben, Simeon, Levi, and Judah

Chapter 30

1. Rachel's maid, Leah's maid, and Leah
2. Issachar and Zebulun
3. Dinah

4. Joseph
5. Because Laban felt blessed in the presence of Jacob
6. All the spotted and speckled sheep and goats
7. Rods of green poplar, hazel, and chestnut trees

Chapter 31

1. God
2. His household idols
3. In the "furniture" (saddle) of a camel
4. Twenty

Chapter 32

1. If Esau attacked him, one company would be able to escape
2. As a peace treaty
3. God himself
4. It shrank

Chapter 33

1. He hugged him, kissed him, and cried
2. Because Jacob's people and flocks were tired and weary
3. Shalem
4. The sons of Hamor

Chapter 34

1. Lay with her and defiled (raped) her
2. They were grieved and extremely angry
3. Hamor
4. Their sons marry each other's daughters and all live in the same land
5. They be circumcised
6. Killed them

Chapter 35

1. Bethel, in the land of Canaan
2. Israel
3. One who struggles/wrestles with God
4. Giving birth
5. Benjamin
6. Bilhah, his father's concubine
7. 180 years old
8. Esau and Jacob

Chapter 36

1. Canaan
2. Edom
3. Esau

Chapter 37

1. Because he was the son of Jacob's old age
2. A coat of many colors
3. Because they envied him and were jealous
4. Bowed down to him
5. Kill him
6. Reuben
7. Sold him into slavery
8. Egypt
9. He was killed by an evil beast

Chapter 38

1. God
2. Shelah
3. Two

Chapter 39

1. Egypt
2. Potiphar
3. Overseer
4. To lie together
5. He refused
6. She accused him of trying to sleep with her
7. Prison
8. He was put in charge of all the prisoners

Chapter 40

1. Pharaoh's chief butler and chief baker
2. He would be released from prison in three days
3. He would be hung in three days
4. To mention Joseph and his situation to Pharaoh

Chapter 41

1. Two
2. There would be seven years of plenty and seven years of famine in the land
3. Save one-fifth of the produce (grain) in the years of plenty to use in the years of famine
4. Pharaoh
5. Thirty years old

Chapter 42

1. Benjamin
2. Because they feared a calamity might befall him
3. Governor
4. Spies
5. Put them in prison
6. Three days
7. Because they had treated Joseph terribly
8. Simeon

Chapter 43

1. After their grain ran out
2. Money for grain
3. Because they feared being accused of taking the money they had brought to make their first grain purchase
4. He wept
5. They were seated according to their ages and birthrights
6. He gave him more of everything compared to his other brothers

Chapter 44

1. His silver cup
2. His personal servant
3. Tore their clothes
4. He would die in grief

Chapter 45

1. They were shocked and in fear
2. God
3. Pharaoh

Chapter 46

1. God
2. Asenath
3. Egypt
4. Goshen

Chapter 47

1. With livestock
2. By selling land to Joseph
3. Seventeen years
4. Not to bury him in Egypt

Chapter 48

1. Manasseh and Ephraim
2. The youngest one, Ephraim
3. One portion more than his brothers

Chapter 49

1. He would not excel
2. He defiled his father's bed
3. They would be divided and scattered
4. He would receive praise from his brothers
5. Joseph
6. In the cave of Machpelah
7. Abraham, Sarah, Isaac, Rebekah, and Leah

Chapter 50

1. Joseph would make them pay for all the harm they had done to him
2. Because he had already forgiven his brothers
3. Deliver his bones out of Egypt

SECTION 3: THE BIBLE BRILLIANT SECTION

45. Group 1

1. Forty years (1 Kings 11:42)
2. They will inherit the earth (Matthew 5:5)
3. A den of thieves (Luke 19:46)
4. His father-in-law (John 18:13)
5. Water turned into blood (Exodus 7:21)
6. Psalm 23 (Psalm 23:2)
7. Tabitha (Dorcas) (Acts 9:40)
8. Visiting the fatherless and widows, and keeping oneself unspotted from the world (James 1:27)
9. Seven (Revelation 1:11)
10. On the twelve gates (Revelation 21:12)
11. A bridegroom (Matthew 25:1)
12. Interpreted his dreams (Daniel 2)
13. They rebuked them (Matthew 19:13)
14. By a well in the land of Midian (Exodus 2:16–21)
15. David
16. Samaritan (Luke 17:16)
17. An earthquake (Acts 16:26)
18. A fleece (Judges 6:37)
19. A crown of twelve stars (Revelation 12:1)
20. Midnight (Acts 16:25)
21. Samuel (1 Samuel 16:13)
22. God and your neighbor (Luke 10:27)
23. King Solomon (Matthew 6:28–29)
24. "Go ye therefore, and teach all nations, baptizing them in the name of the Father, and of the Son, and of the Holy Ghost" (Matthew 28:19)
25. Wrath (Proverbs 15:1)
26. He was killed after David instructed his men to abandon Uriah during a battle (2 Samuel 11:15)
27. Lameness (Acts 3:2)
28. Vegetables and water (Daniel 1:12)
29. He was circumcised (Luke 2:21)
30. Barabbas (Matthew 27:21)
31. Levi (Numbers 18:20–24)
32. As a sign that God had sent him (Exodus 4:6–8)
33. Two nations (Genesis 25:23)
34. He rested (Genesis 2:1–3)
35. Do not judge them and treat them impartially (James 2:1–4)
36. Jerusalem (Ezra 6:3)
37. "And thou shalt love the Lord thy God with all they heart, and with all they soul, and with all thy mind, and with all thy strength: this is the first commandment" (Mark 12:29–30)
38. A shining light from heaven (Acts 9:3)
39. Pig feeder (Luke 15:15)
40. None (Acts 27:22, 44)
41. In prison (Philemon 1:23)
42. Gilead (Jeremiah 46:11)
43. Saul (Acts 7:58)
44. The good Samaritan (Luke 10:29)
45. In spirit and truth (John 4:23–24)

46. Forty days (Jonah 3:4)
47. Ten (Exodus 7:14–12:30)
48. Fisherman (Matthew 4:21)
49. Timothy (2 Timothy 3:15)
50. John the Baptist (Matthew 3:1–2)

46. Group 2

1. The love of money (1 Timothy 6:10)
2. Potiphar (Genesis 37:36)
3. Isaiah (Acts 8:30)
4. Ananias (Acts 9:17)
5. Lazarus (John 11:41)
6. Aaron's rod swallowed them (Exodus 7:12)
7. Raised him from the dead (2 Kings 4:32–37)
8. "Put her away privily" (divorce her quietly) (Matthew 1:19)
9. Let the mother bird go free (Deuteronomy 22:6–7)
10. Tarsus (Acts 21:39)
11. Calvary or Golgotha (place of a skull) (John 19:17)
12. Paul (1 Corinthians 13:11)
13. Timothy (Philemon 1:1)
14. A lion (Proverbs 19:12)
15. Egypt (Matthew 2:13–14)
16. A parcel of land (Ruth 4:3)
17. Ten male donkeys and ten female donkeys laden with goods from Egypt (Genesis 45:23)
18. "Blessed is the man that walketh not in the counsel of the ungodly" (Psalm 1:1)
19. A ladder (Genesis 28:12)
20. Titus
21. Samson (Judges 16:5–6)
22. Levi (Deuteronomy 10:9)
23. Pharaoh's daughter (Exodus 2:5)
24. Obed (Ruth 4:17)
25. Cattle (Genesis 13:2)
26. A stone (Daniel 2:34)
27. Bethany (John 11:1)
28. Jacob and Rachel (Genesis 46:19)
29. They were killed by two bears (2 Kings 2:24)
30. A fever (Matthew 8:14)
31. Mahlon and Chilion (Ruth 1:2)
32. Uriah (2 Samuel 11:3)
33. You are guilty of breaking the whole law (James 2:10)
34. A double portion (2 Kings 2:9)
35. The death of Herod (Matthew 2:15)
36. A lion (Judges 14:6)
37. A viper snake (Acts 28:3)
38. Ahab (1 Kings 21:16)
39. Canaan (Genesis 17:8)
40. Herodias (Matthew 14:8)
41. Rachel (Genesis 31:32)
42. They wouldn't bow down to Nebuchadnezzar's golden image (Daniel 3:11–12)
43. Forty (Acts 1:3)
44. The Word of God (Luke 8:11)
45. One (Luke 17:15)
46. He was cast into darkness (Matthew 22:13)
47. Boaz (Ruth 4:13)
48. They were all left-handed (Judges 20:16)
49. Augustus Caesar (Luke 2:1)
50. They saw a star in the east (Matthew 2:2)

47. Group 3

1. Wisdom and instruction (Proverbs 1:7)
2. His long hair (Judges 16:17)
3. Red Sea (Exodus 13:18)
4. A rich man entering the kingdom of heaven (Matthew 19:24)
5. Forty (Joshua 5:6)
6. Good fruit (Matthew 7:17)
7. The tongue (James 3:5)
8. With animal sacrifices (Leviticus 4)
9. Patiently (James 5:7)
10. By his own lust (James 1:14)
11. Judah (Micah 5:2)
12. Patmos (Revelation 1:9)
13. Donkey (Numbers 22:28)
14. Jordan River (2 Kings 5:10)
15. Herod (Luke 23:7)
16. There was a famine in Canaan (Genesis 47:4)
17. Rivers of water (Psalm 1:1–3)
18. Beasts (Daniel 7:3)
19. Without ceasing (1 Thessalonians 5:17)
20. He went mad and lived as a beast (Daniel 4:33–36)
21. Malachi
22. Walking on water (John 6:19–20)
23. A famine (Genesis 12:10)
24. Warming himself by a fire (John 18:25)
25. Because only God could forgive sins (Mark 2:7)
26. A servant was sent back to Mesopotamia to choose a wife from Isaac's own family (Genesis 24)
27. One hundred years old (Genesis 21:5)
28. People who hear God's Word but have it choked out by concern for the world (Matthew 13:22)
29. He sat down on the east side of the city and built a booth (shelter) (Jonah 4:5)
30. He was thrown into the lions' den (Daniel 6:10, 16)
31. The walls fell down (Joshua 6:20)
32. Lot (Genesis 12:5)
33. Tarshish (Jonah 1:3)
34. Timothy (2 Timothy 1:5)
35. His foreign wives turned his heart toward idolatry (1 Kings 11:4)
36. The prodigal son (Luke 15:23–24)
37. That he was not sinful like other men (Luke 18:11)
38. Judah (1 Kings 11:31–36; 12:20–21)
39. They spread news about Jesus's birth (Luke 2:17)
40. "For his mercy endureth for ever"
41. He was angry (Jonah 4:1)
42. Gethsemane (Matthew 26:36)
43. Simon of Cyrene (Matthew 27:32)
44. Phoebe (Romans 16:1–2)
45. Amittai (Jonah 1:1)
46. Rehoboam (1 Kings 11:43)
47. Seventy times seven (Matthew 18:22)
48. Nazareth (Matthew 2:23)
49. Ararat (Genesis 8:4)
50. For her sons to sit on Jesus's right and left hands in the kingdom (Matthew 20:21)

48. Group 4

1. His nephew (Genesis 14:12)
2. Abram (Genesis 12:1)
3. Nehemiah (Nehemiah 2:17)
4. Samuel's (1 Samuel 2:19)
5. John (Luke 1:13)
6. As one having authority (Matthew 7:29)
7. As a little child (Luke 18:17)
8. An olive leaf (Genesis 8:11)
9. Is it lawful for a man to put away (divorce) his wife? (Matthew 19:3)
10. Marriage and divorce (Matthew 19:6)
11. Deborah (Judges 5:7)
12. Ehud (Judges 3:15–25)
13. Ephraim and Manasseh (Joshua 14:4)
14. Peter (Acts 3:6)
15. John the Baptist (Luke 7:28)
16. Works (James 2:17)
17. They were swallowed up by the earth (Numbers 16:1–35)
18. With fear and trembling (Philippians 2:12)
19. Twenty-seven
20. He tore down his barns and built larger barns (Luke 12:18)
21. "Thy kingdom come" (Matthew 6:10)
22. Sixth (Luke 1:26)
23. 120 talents of gold, spices, and precious stones (1 Kings 10:10)
24. They were cast into the lake of fire (Revelation 20:15)
25. Go with them two miles (Matthew 5:41)
26. Love (1 Peter 4:8)
27. Take no thought for it (Matthew 6:34)
28. The old bottles will burst (Luke 5:37)
29. Yeast (Matthew 13:33)
30. Charge it to Paul (Philemon 1:18)
31. Sleeping (Jonah 1:5)
32. Rebekah (Genesis 24:67)
33. Matthias (Acts 1:26)
34. Lodged in its branches (Matthew 13:32)
35. The heart (Proverbs 13:12)
36. Oil (Matthew 25:3)
37. East (Genesis 2:8)
38. Thirty-nine
39. The butler and the baker (Genesis 40:5)
40. Jerusalem (Matthew 2:3)
41. Turtledoves or pigeons (Leviticus 5:7)
42. The wood (Genesis 22:6)
43. Money for grain and a silver cup (Genesis 44:2)
44. The field of blood (Acts 1:19)
45. Sarah (Genesis 17:15)
46. Its mother's milk (Exodus 23:19)
47. A sharp sword (Revelation 19:15)
48. Esther (Esther 3:1)
49. Salt (Matthew 5:13)
50. He commanded the spirit of divination to leave her (Acts 16:16–19)

49. Imprisoned

1. B (Acts 16:25–26)
2. C (Acts 5:12–42)
3. D (Matthew 14:2–4)
4. A (Genesis 39:1–20)

5. D (Genesis 42:16–17)
6. B (Jeremiah 32:2)
7. C (Jeremiah 52:11)
8. B (2 Chronicles 16:7–10)

9. A (Judges 16:21)
10. B (2 Kings 24:15)
11. D (1 Kings 22:26–27)
12. C (2 Kings 17:4)

51. Fasting

1. D (Matthew 4:2)
2. C (Exodus 34:28)
3. B (1 Kings 17:2–6)
4. B (2 Samuel 12:14–31)
5. C (Acts 23:12–13)

6. A (Acts 27:33–37)
7. A (Daniel 6:16–19)
8. B (Acts 14:23)
9. A (Nehemiah 1:4–2:4)
10. A (Jeremiah 36:8–10)

52. Wine

1. D (Matthew 11:19)
2. C (1 Timothy 5:23)
3. A (1 Timothy 3:3)
4. A (Proverbs 31:6)

5. B (Judges 7:24–25)
6. A (Numbers 6:1–3)
7. B (Matthew 27:34)
8. C (Luke 5:36–39)

53. The Apostles

1. A (Acts 12:2)
2. C (Acts 1:25–26)

3. A (Matthew 9:9–13)
4. D (John 13:23)

54. Kings

1. D (1 Kings 18:17)
2. B (Judges 4:2–3)
3. C (2 Kings 17)
4. A (1 Kings 16:31)
5. A (Numbers 21:1)

6. B (Joshua 11:1–15)
7. D (Deuteronomy 3:11)
8. C (1 Samuel 8:1–21)
9. B (1 Samuel 16:13)
10. B (2 Samuel 12)

55. Heaven Awaits

1. A (John 14:3)
2. C (John 3:3)
3. C (Revelation 21)
4. A (Revelation 3:12)
5. D (Revelation 21:19–20)
6. B (Revelation 21:18)

7. C (Revelation 21:21)
8. A (Revelation 22:2)
9. D (Revelation 4:4)
10. B (Revelation 4:6–11)
11. D (Revelation 21:21)
12. D (Revelation 21)

56. Hairy and Hairless

1. C (Ezekiel 44:20)
2. C (Judges 16:17)
3. B (Acts 21:23–36)

4. B (Daniel 4:33)
5. C (Genesis 9:1–3)
6. D (Job 1:20–21)

7. D (2 Samuel 14:26)
8. C (Leviticus 14:7–9)
9. C (Leviticus 19:27)

10. C (2 Kings 2:23)
11. C (Ezekiel 5:1–4)
12. C (2 Kings 1:8)

57. Encouragement

1. tower, safe
2. Proverbs, Trust, heart
3. Fear, dismayed, hand
4. John, Peace, world
5. John, me, world
6. God, refuge, mountains, sea
7. Timothy, spirit, power, love
8. Psalm, LORD
9. Cast, LORD

10. Peter, care
11. perfect, mind
12. Psalm, LORD, song
13. Psalm, hiding, shield
14. dust, word
15. Psalm, word
16. afflicted, learn
17. Psalm, distress, LORD

58. Friendship

1. friend, brother
2. Proverbs, angry, soul
3. wise, fools
4. better, kisses
5. Two, help
6. John, love

7. friend, brother
8. Iron, man
9. righteous, wicked
10. adulterers, world, enemy
11. friends, tears

SECTION 4: THE BONUS SECTION

59. The Book of Revelation

Chapter 1

1. John
2. Jesus
3. The seven churches in Asia
4. The angels of the seven churches and the seven churches themselves

Chapter 2

1. They had left their first love, God
2. They had no current problem, but their faith would be greatly tested by the upcoming tribulation
3. Pergamos
4. Thyatira

Chapter 3

1. Sardis
2. Philadelphia
3. A lukewarm church

Chapter 4

1. God
2. The seven spirits of God

3. A lion, a calf, a man, and a flying eagle
4. Twenty-four elders

Chapter 5

1. A book sealed with seven seals
2. Jesus

Chapter 6

1. White
2. Wars
3. Famine
4. The pale horse
5. Those slain because of the Word of God
6. A great earthquake

Chapter 7

1. 144,000
2. People of all nations, kindreds, people, and tongues

Chapter 8

1. Judgment upon the earth
2. Hail and fire
3. The burning of a great mountain
4. A great star
5. One-third

Chapter 9

1. Torment them without killing them
2. Four angels that killed a third of humankind
3. Two hundred million
4. No, they did not

Chapter 10

1. That God's plan would no longer be delayed
2. It would be finished

Chapter 11

1. Forty-two months (three and a half years)

2. They prophesied about the coming judgment of God
3. The beast of the bottomless pit
4. They ascended to heaven
5. The establishment of the kingdom of God on earth

Chapter 12

1. Israel
2. Satan
3. Satan
4. Jesus
5. The ones who "keep the commandments of God, and have the testimony of Jesus Christ"

Chapter 13

1. A leopard
2. Make war with the saints
3. A beast with two horns
4. Their right hands or their foreheads

Chapter 14

1. The 144,000 survivors of the tribulation
2. The gospel to all people
3. The second angel
4. The mark of the beast
5. A cloud

Chapter 15

1. The survivors of the tribulation and those who refused the mark of the beast
2. The seven last plagues of God's wrath, reserved for those left on earth

Chapter 16

1. Horrible sores for the people
2. Blood
3. Blood
4. Excessive heat from the sun

5. Darkness

6. Euphrates River

7. A great earthquake

Chapter 17

1. The seven kingdoms that would come into power

2. The ten kings and their nations that would support the beast

Chapter 18

1. One hour

2. A millstone

Chapter 19

1. Babylon

2. Jesus

3. They were cast into the lake of fire

Chapter 20

1. The bottomless pit for one thousand years

2. Resurrection

3. He was cast into the lake of fire

4. The lost and the remainder of the dead

Chapter 21

1. Heaven and earth

2. The new heaven

3. The twelve tribes of Israel

4. The length, width, and height were all equal to 12,000 furlongs (1,380 miles)

5. Jasper

6. Pearls

7. The glory of God

Chapter 22

1. A river of water of life

2. The tree of life

3. Blessing

4. Amen

60. Crossword Puzzle 2

Timothy E. Parker is a Guinness World Records Puzzle Master and an ordained minister. He entertains over twenty million puzzle solvers as the senior crossword puzzle editor of the Universal line of crosswords and assorted puzzle games. He is the author of more than thirty books and the founder of Bible Brilliant. CNN calls his puzzles "Smart games for smart people," and he has created custom games for companies including Microsoft, Disney, Coca-Cola, Nike, Warner Bros., and Comcast. For more Bible puzzles and quizzes, go to www.BibleBrilliant.com.